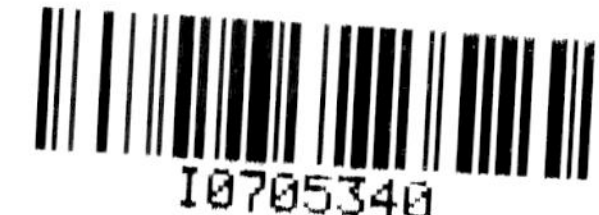

CUTE CHRISTMAS SNOW GLOBES

Coloring Book

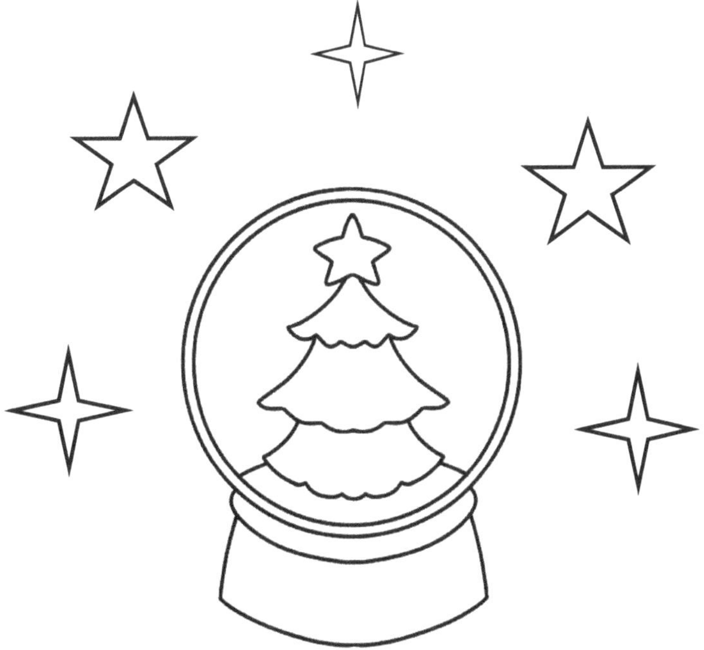

¡WELCOME!

TO THIS EXTRAORDINARY
MAGICAL
WORLD FULL OF COLORS.

NAME: ________________

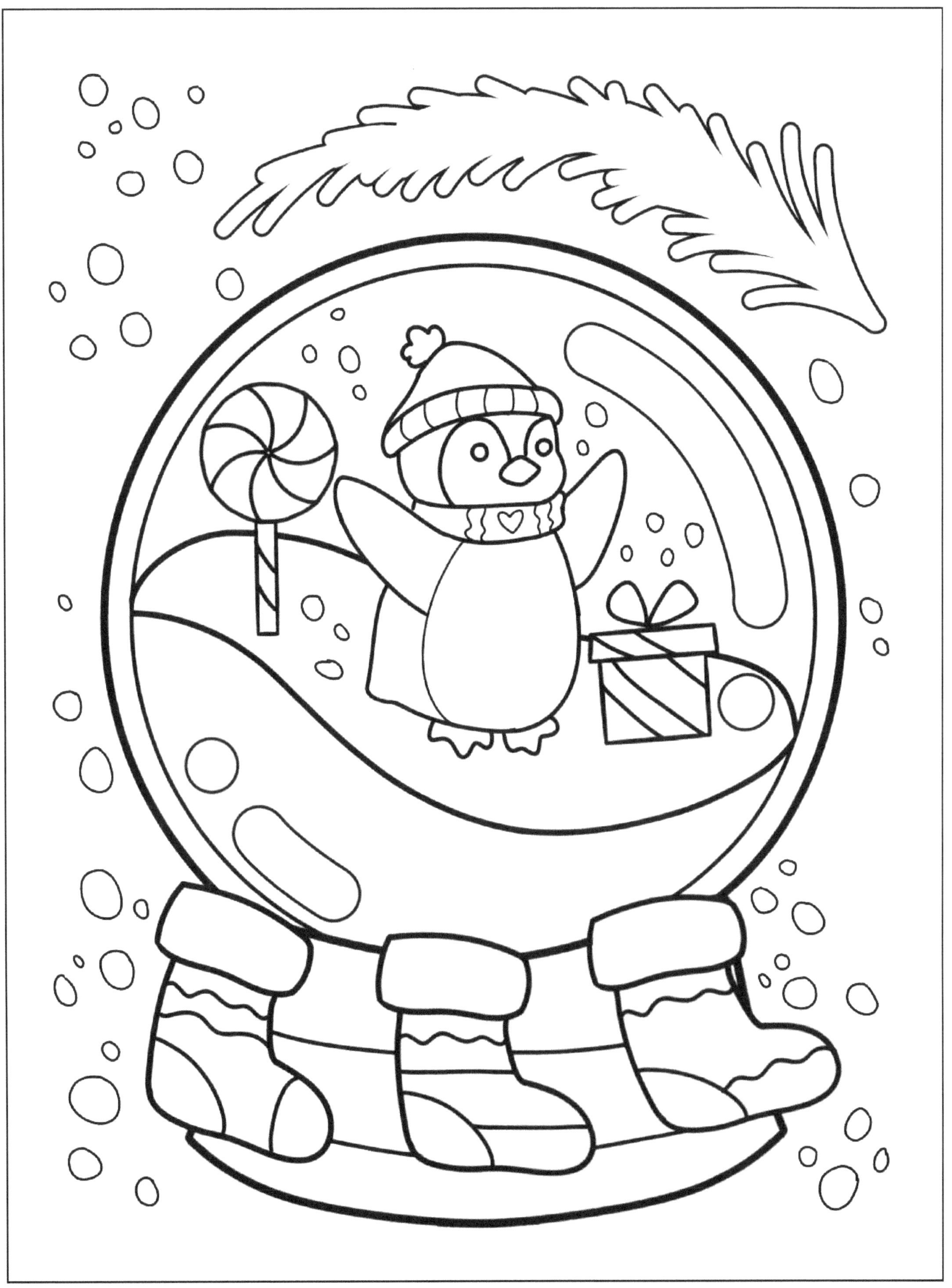

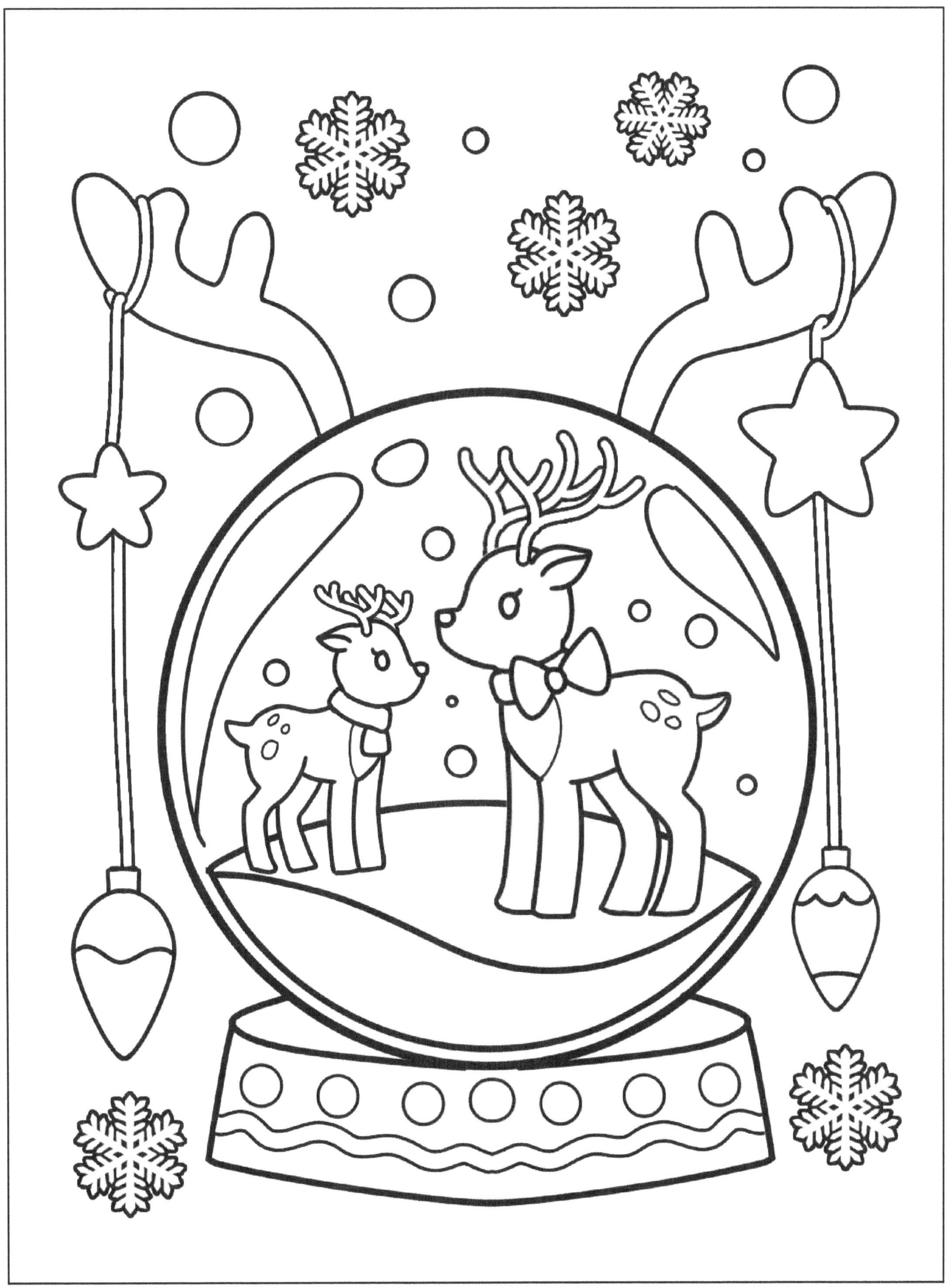

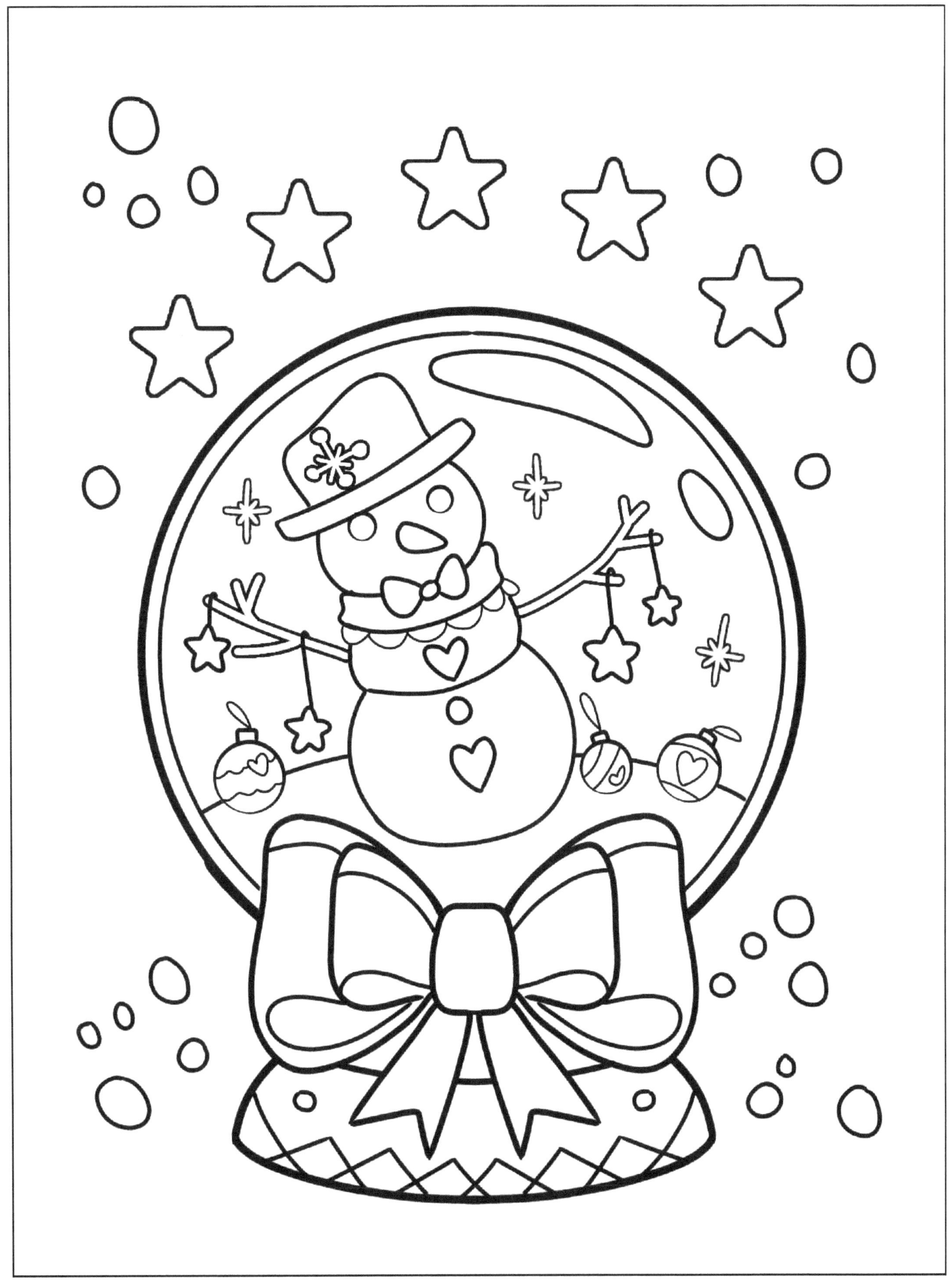

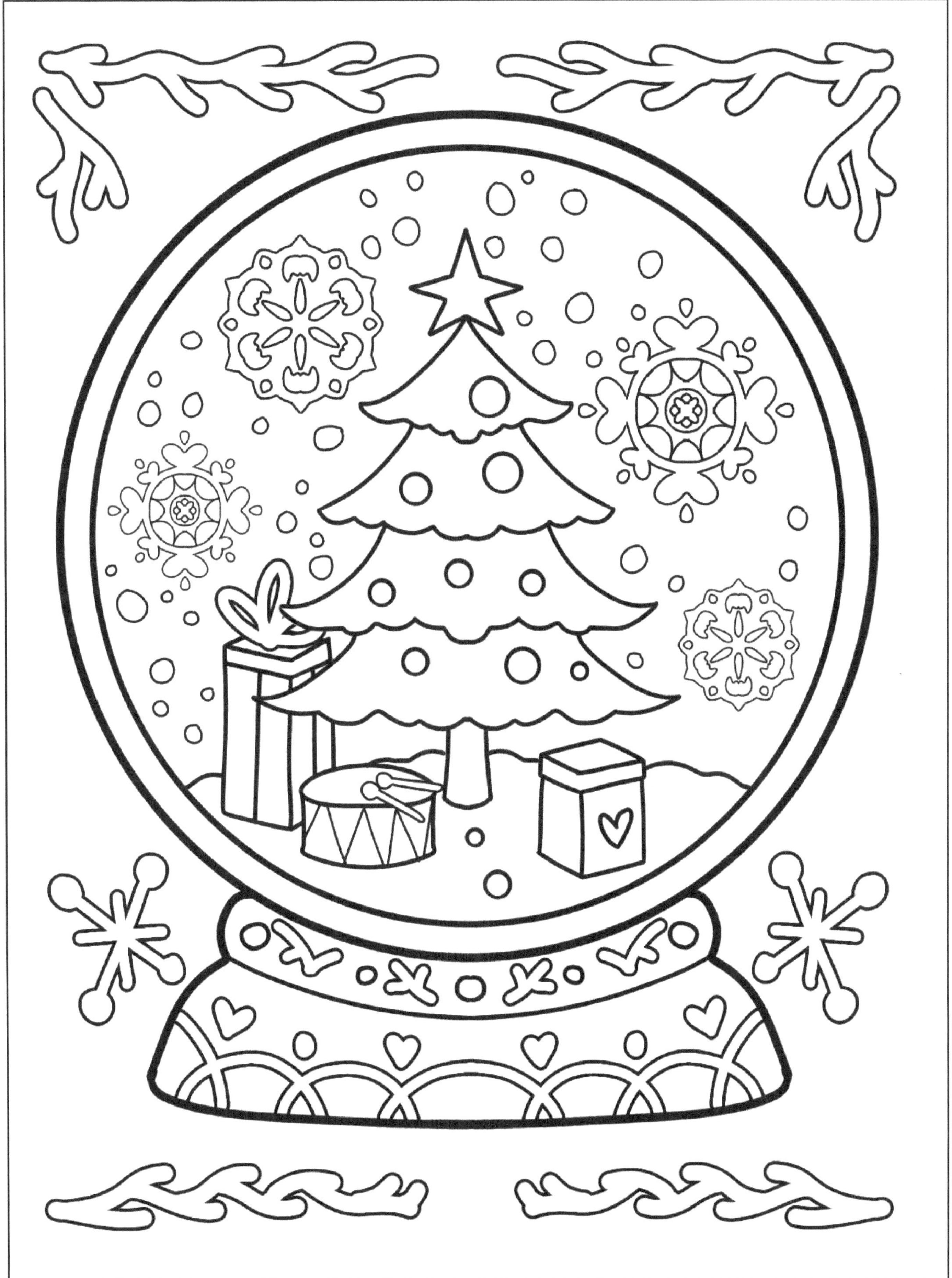

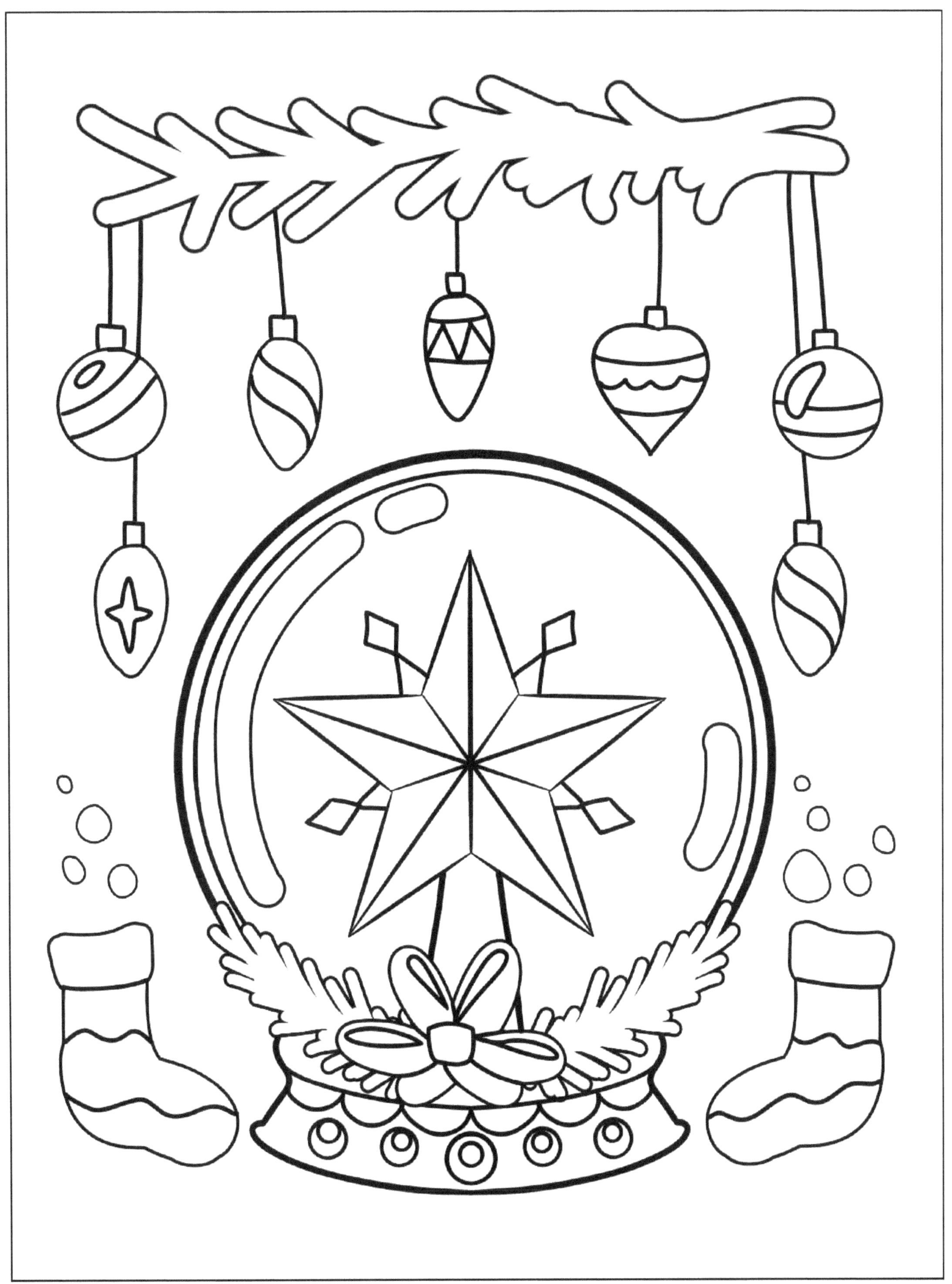

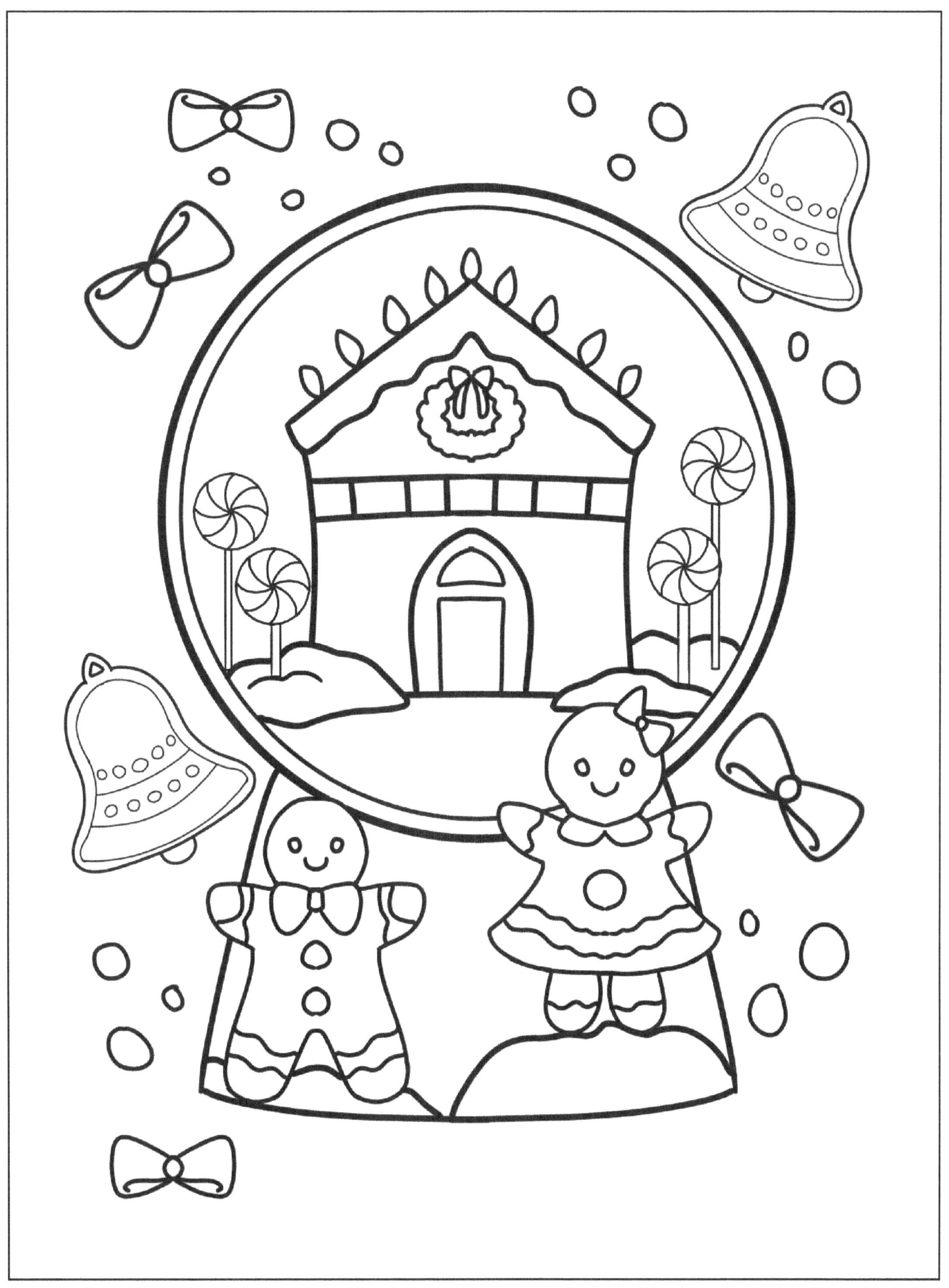

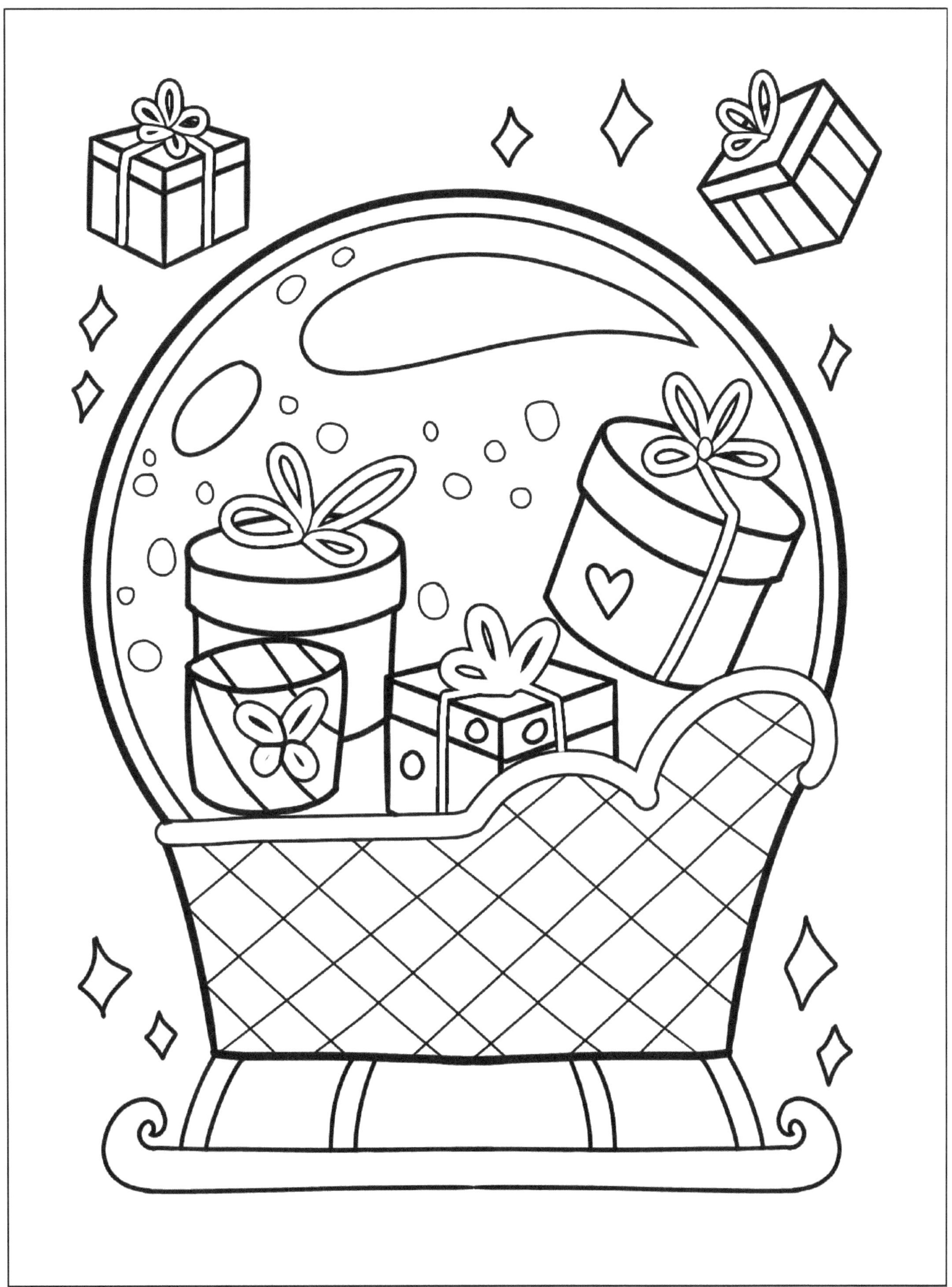

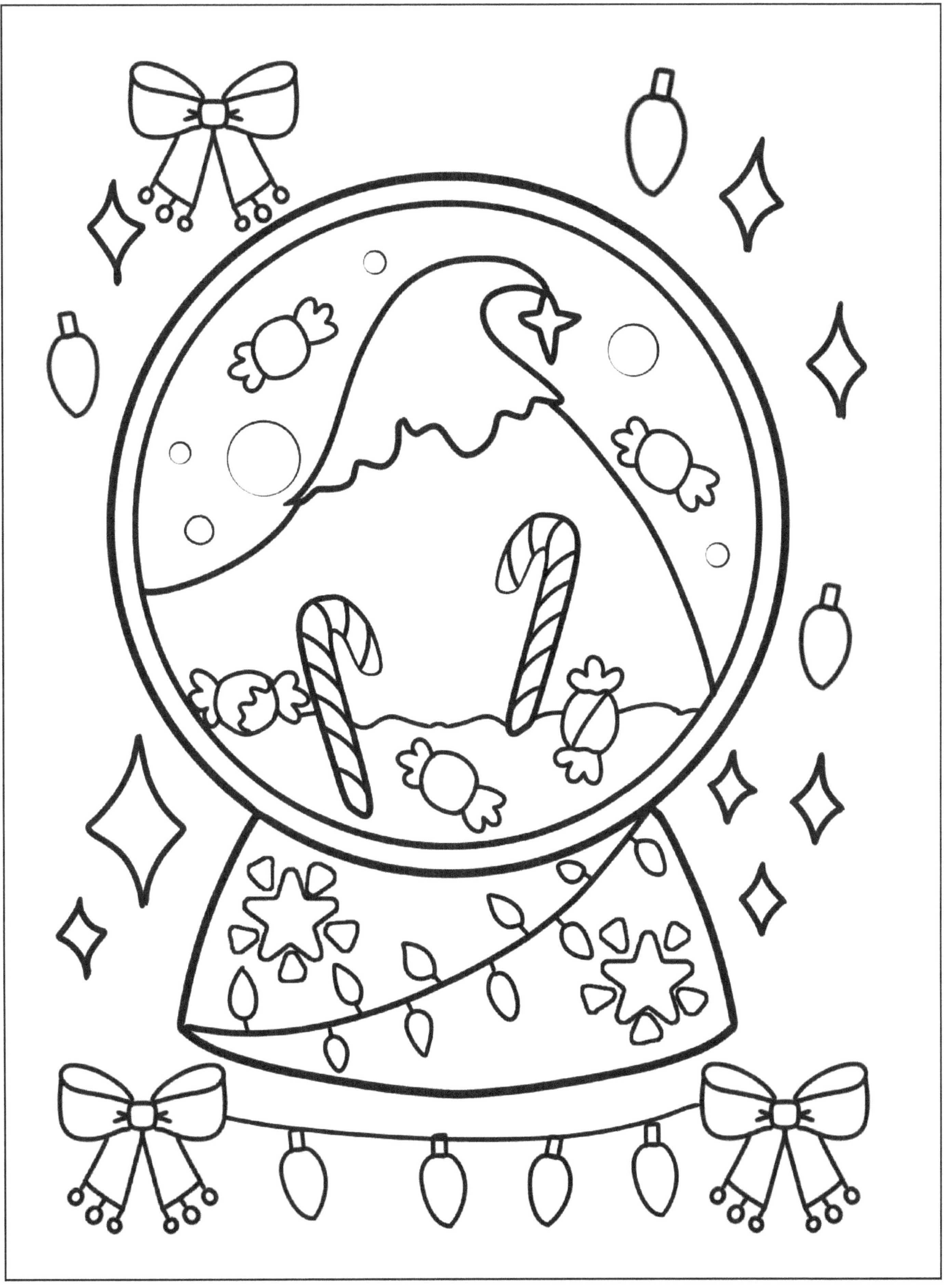

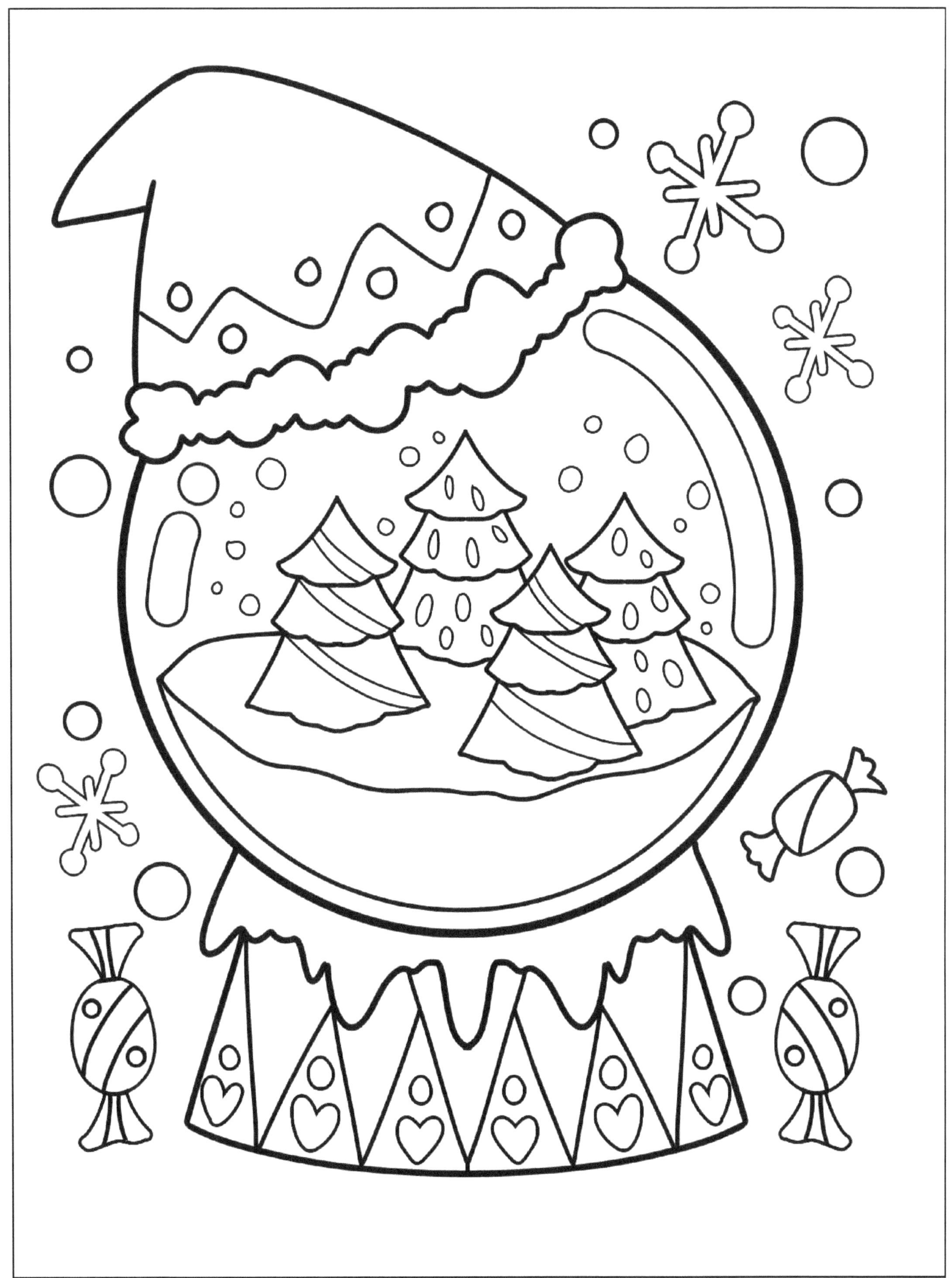

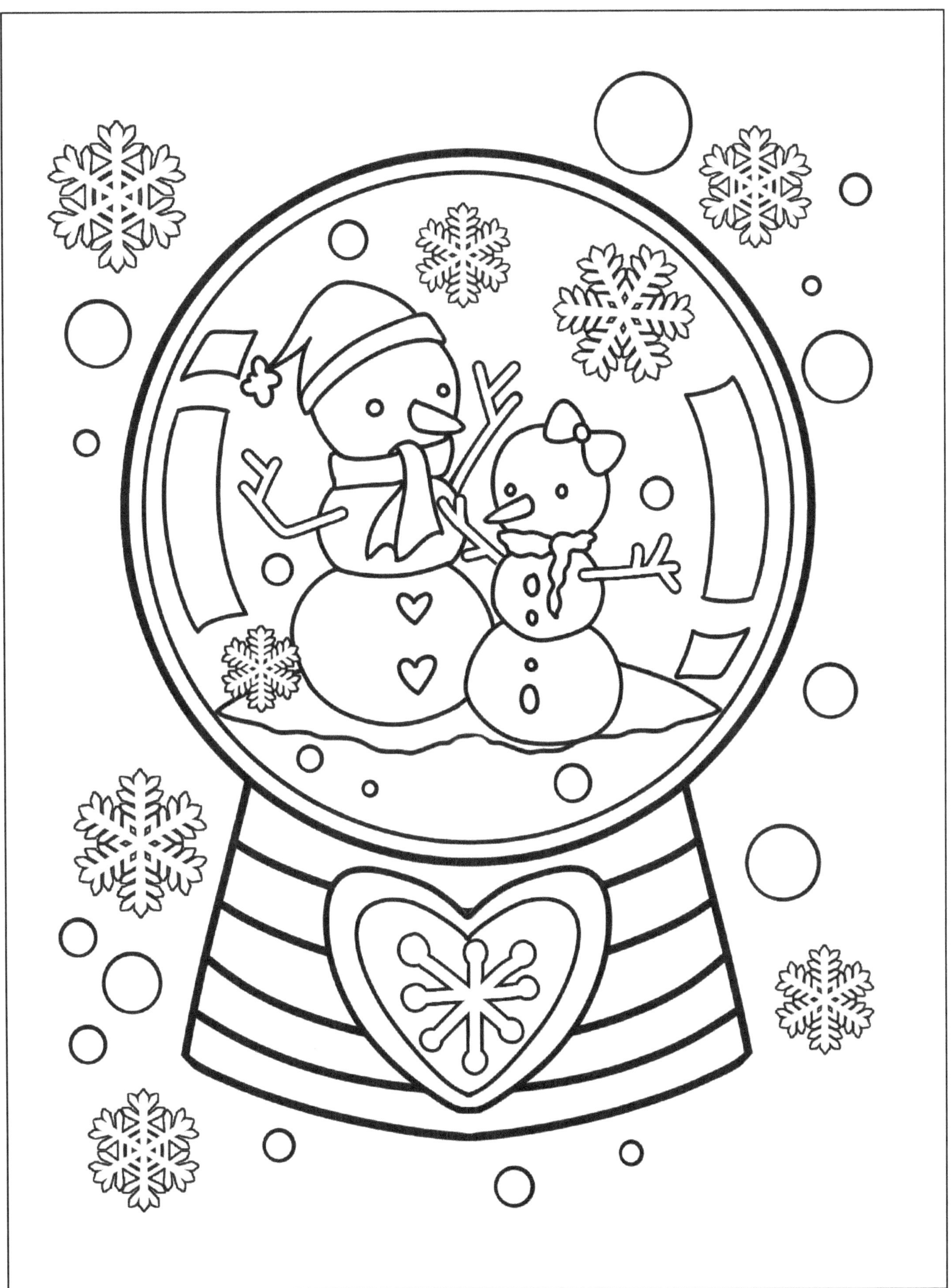

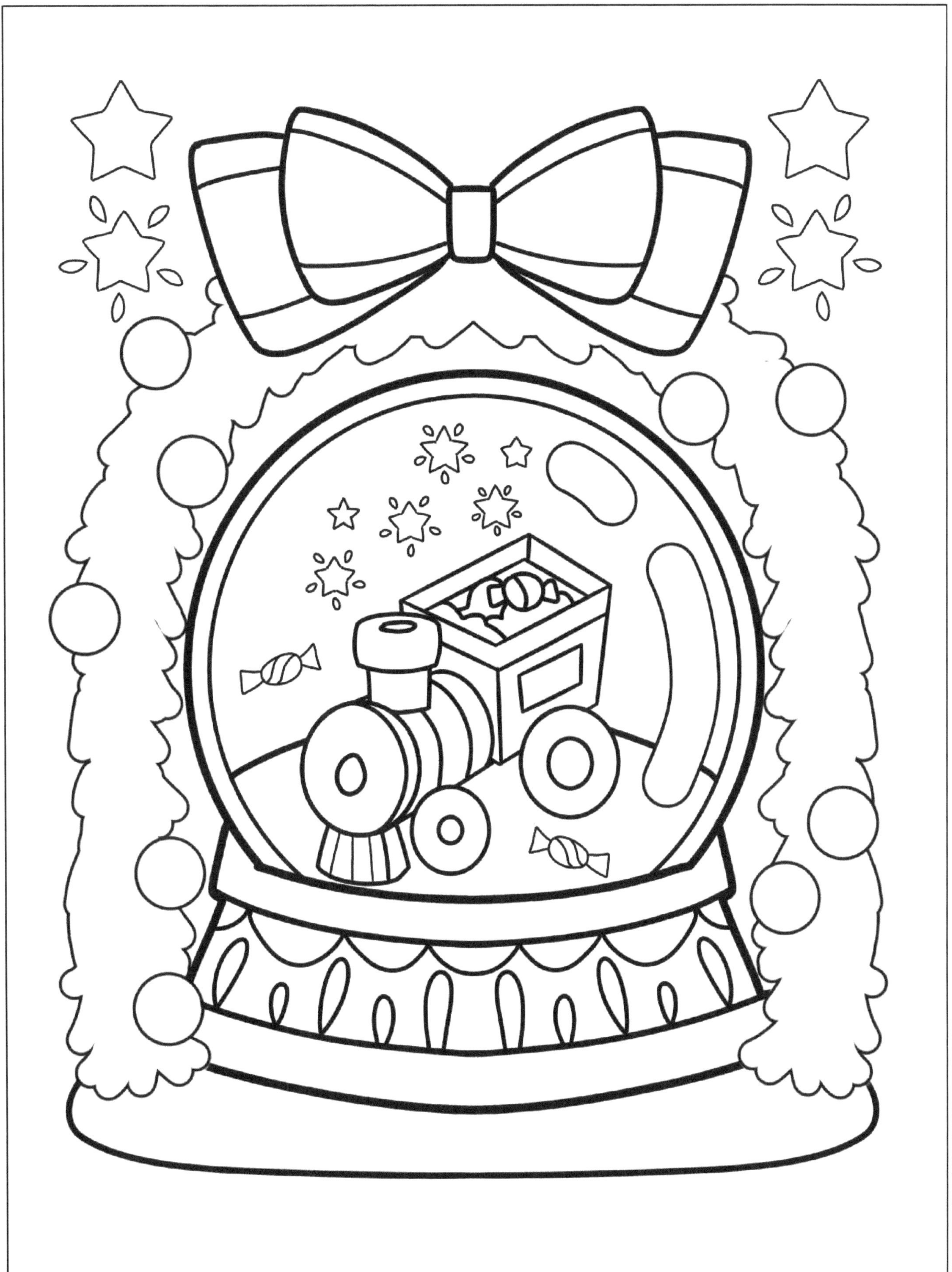

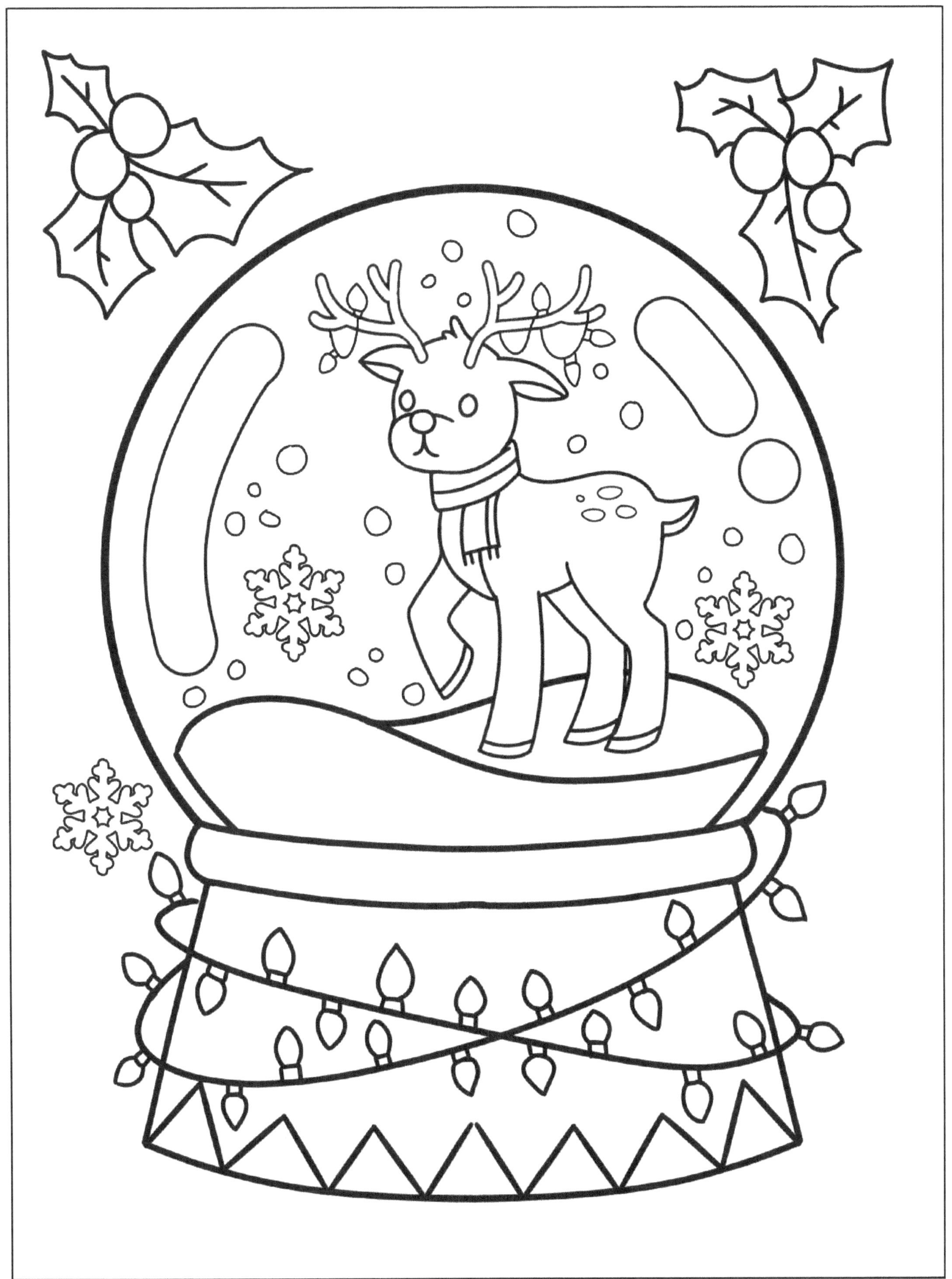

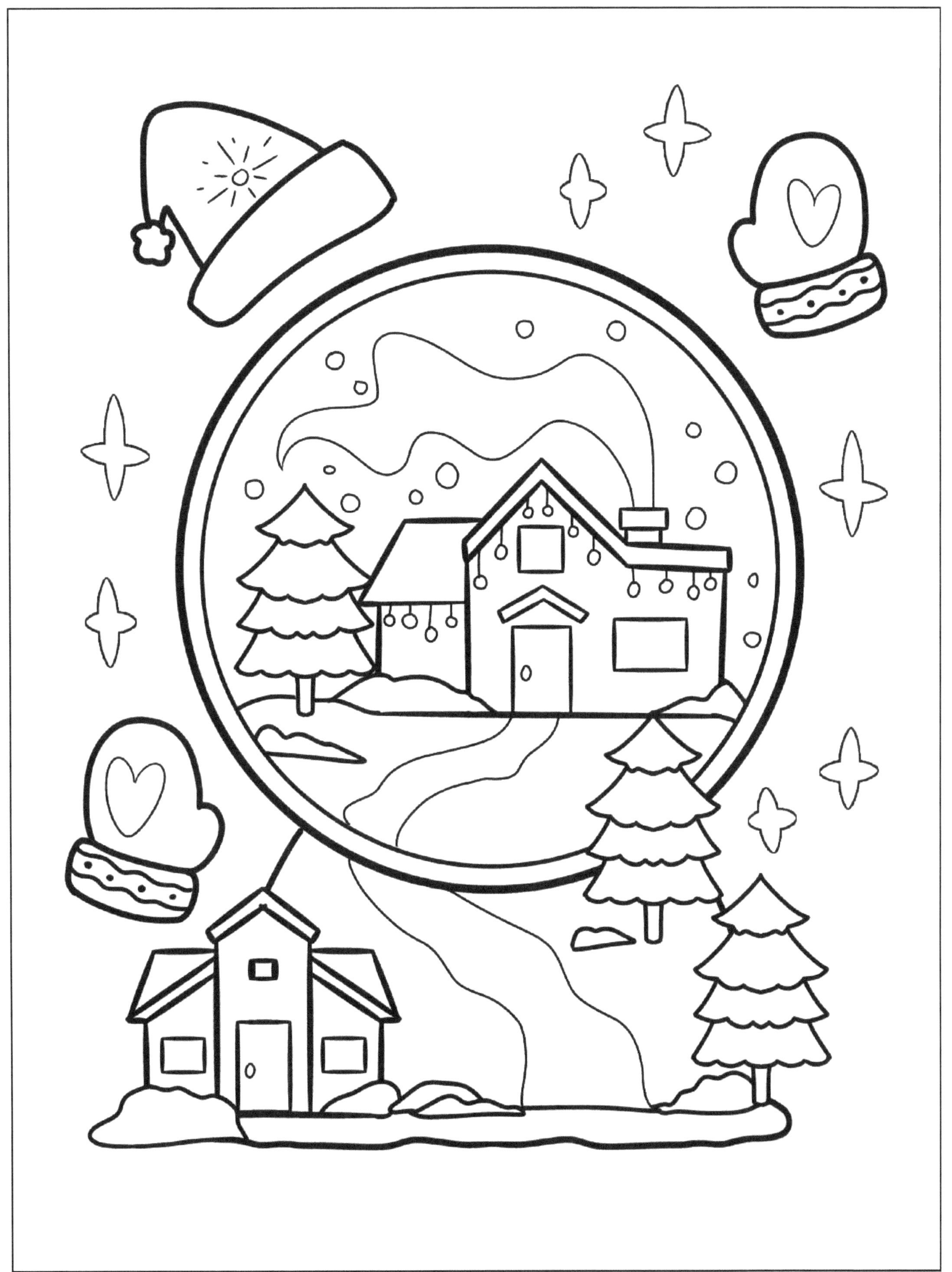

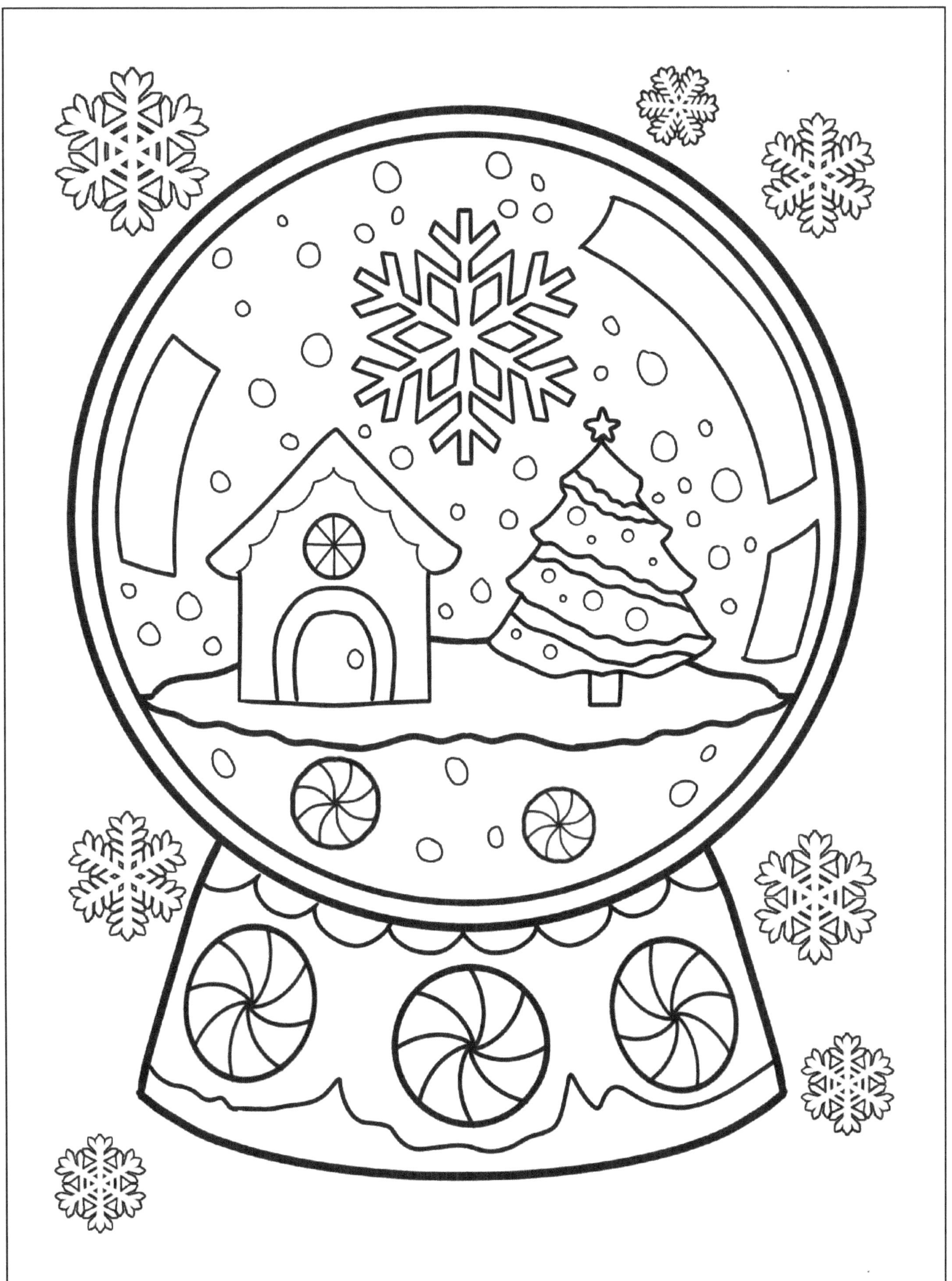

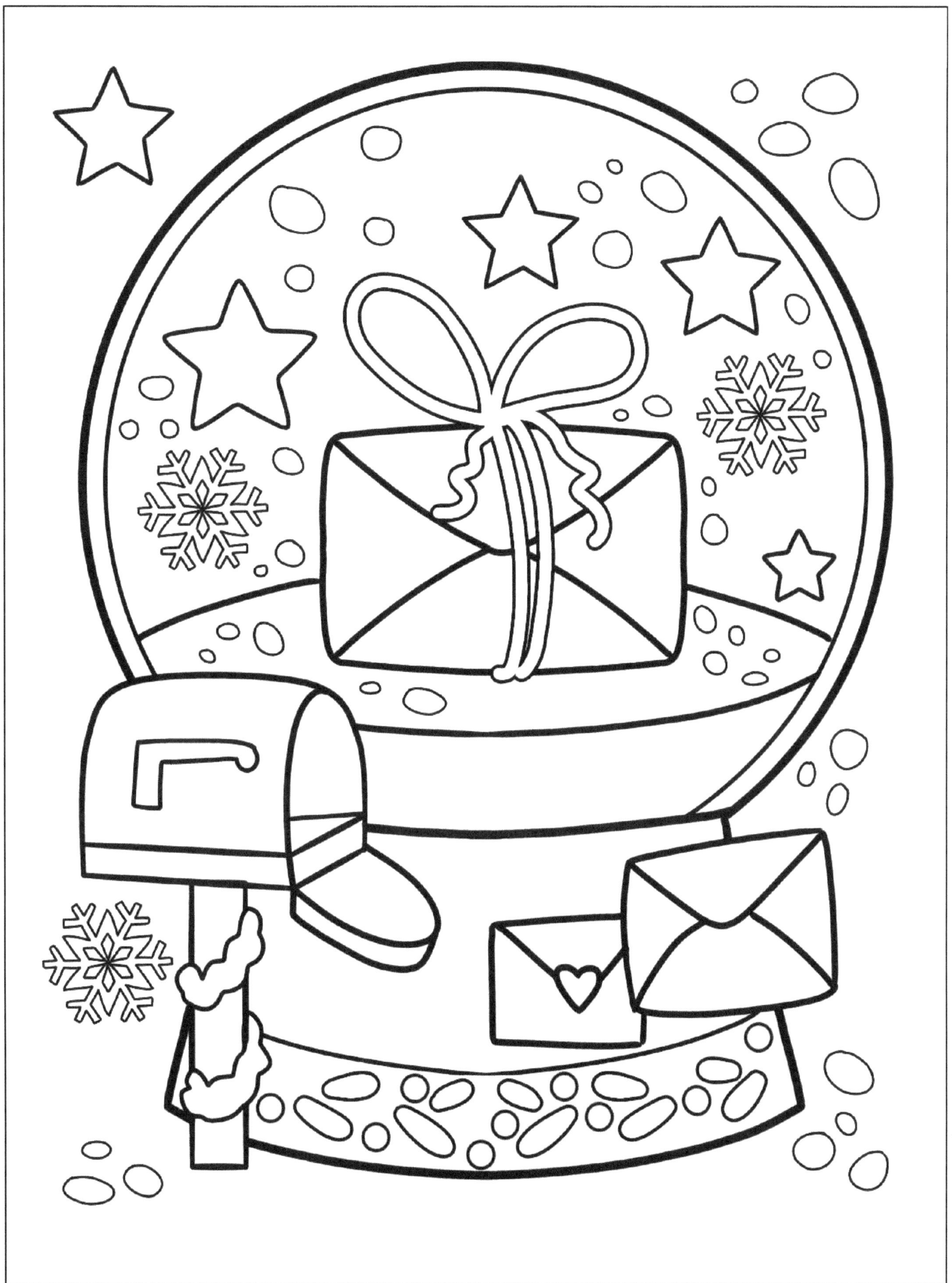

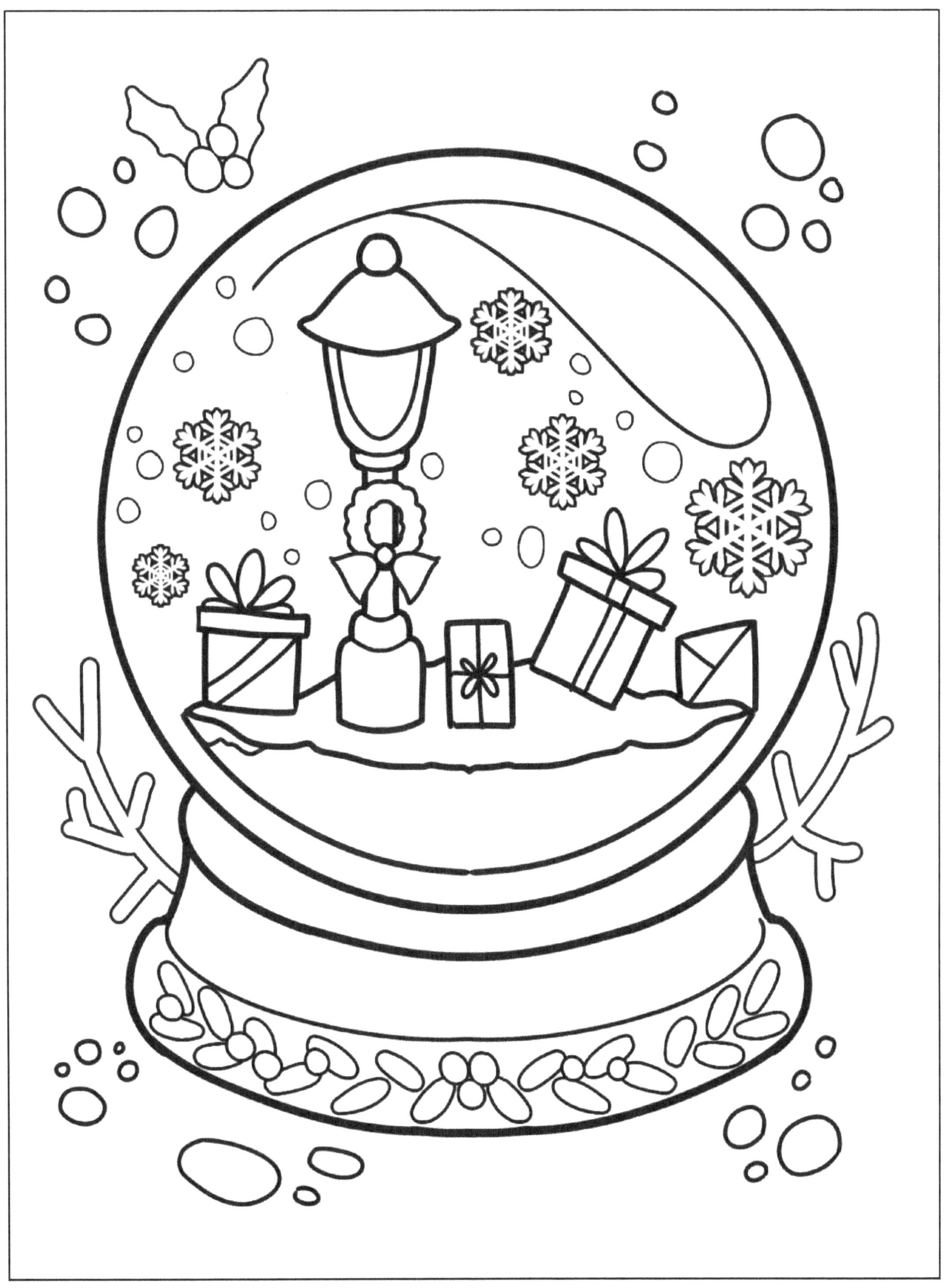

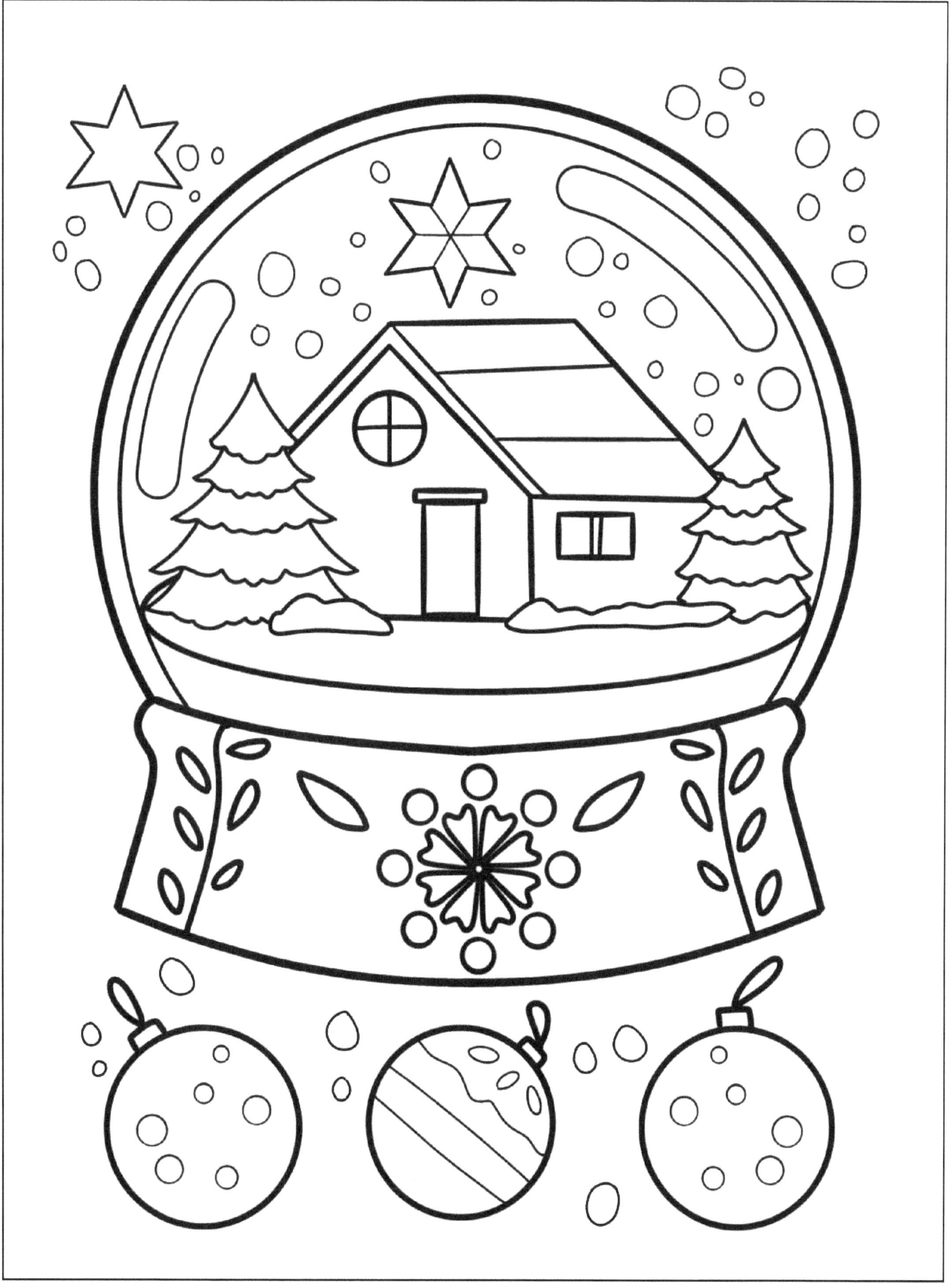

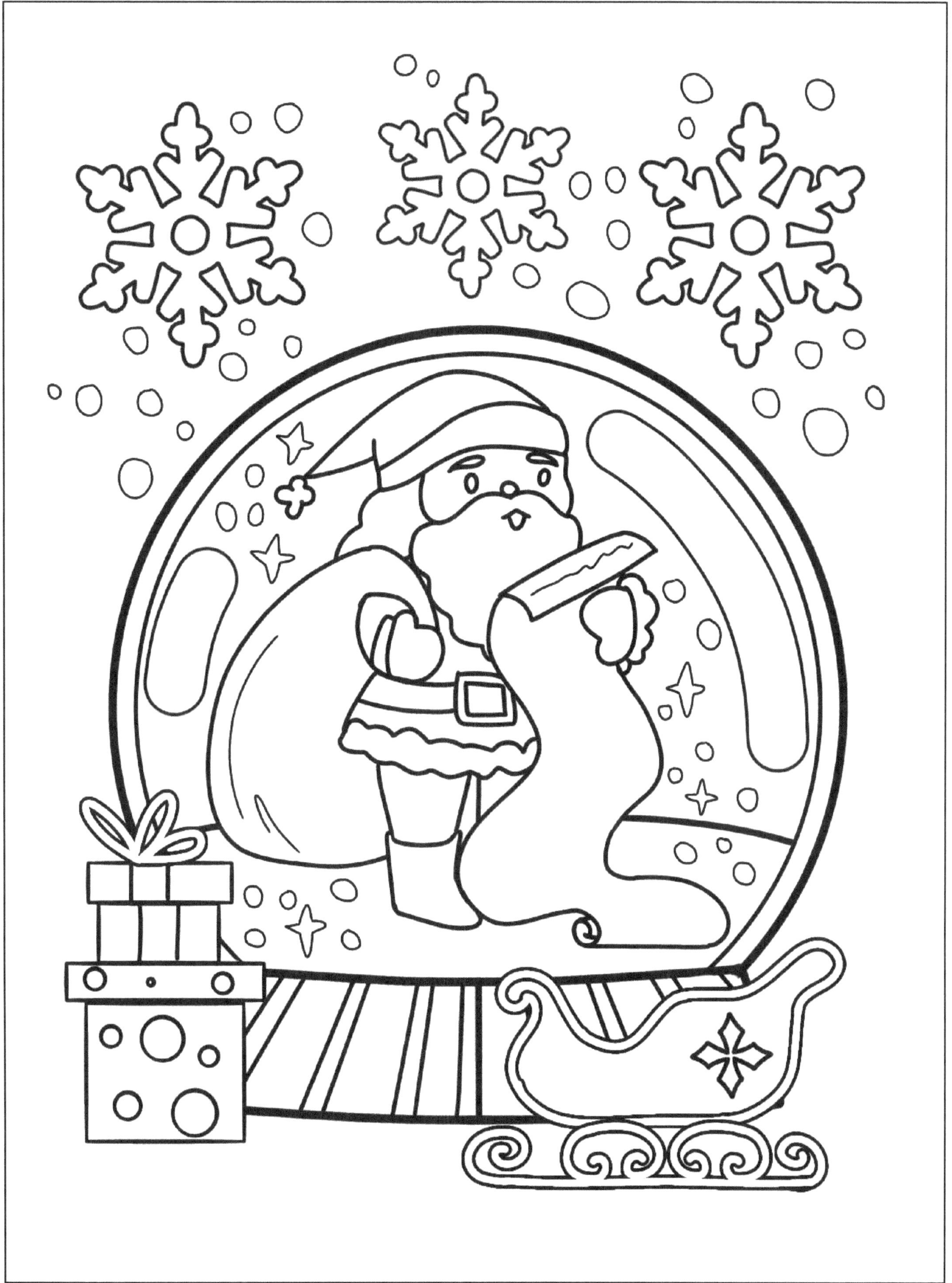

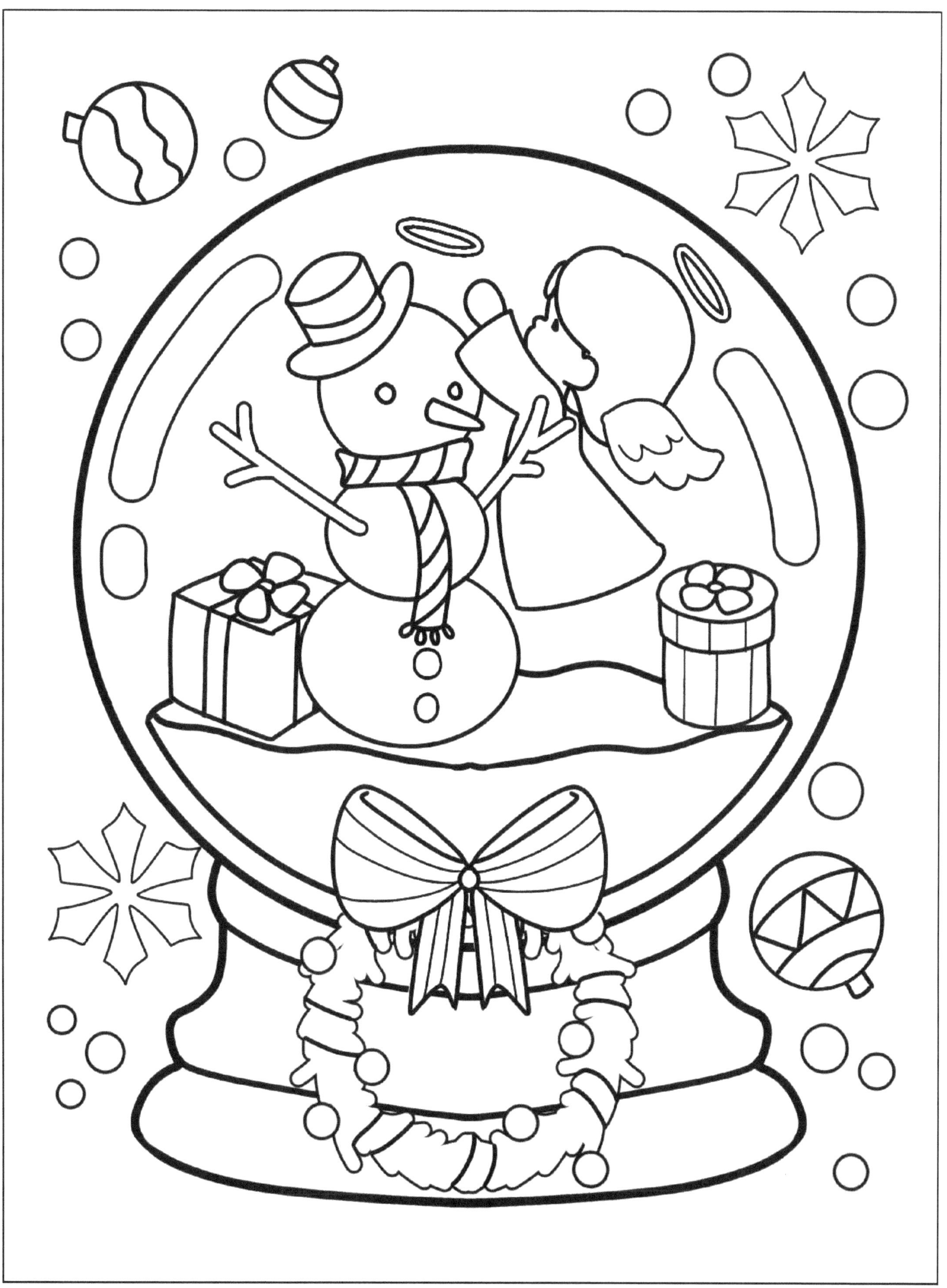

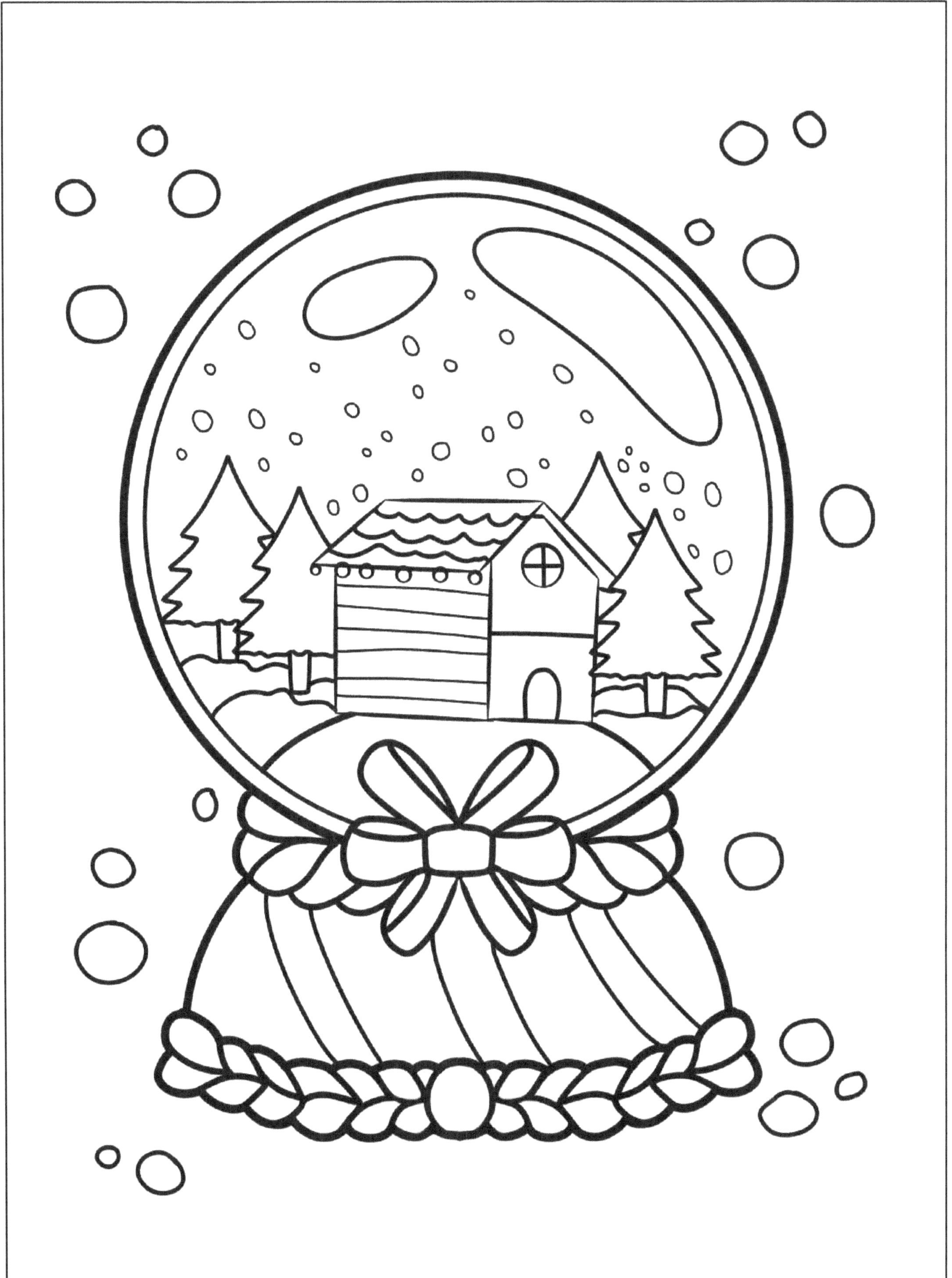

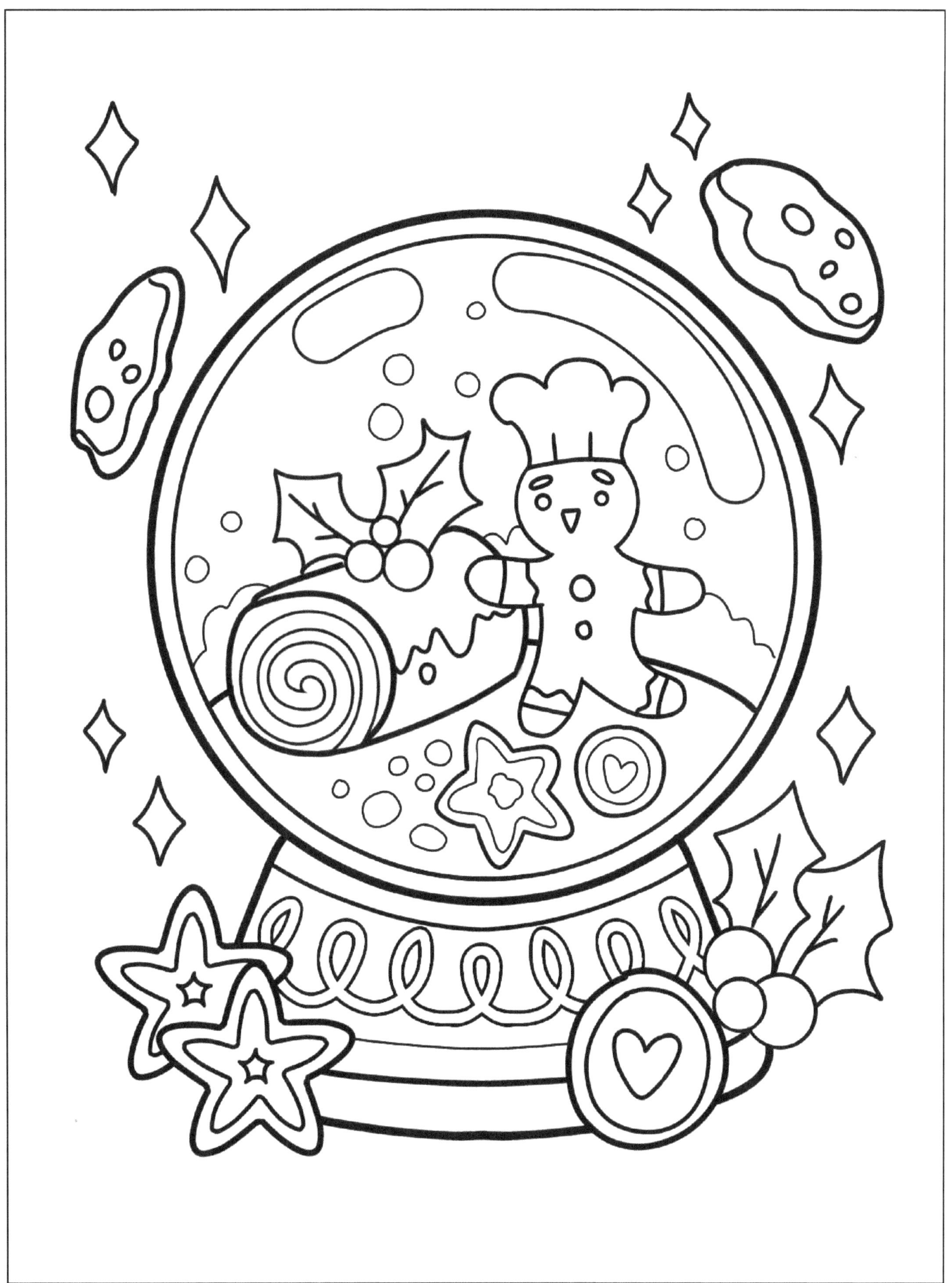

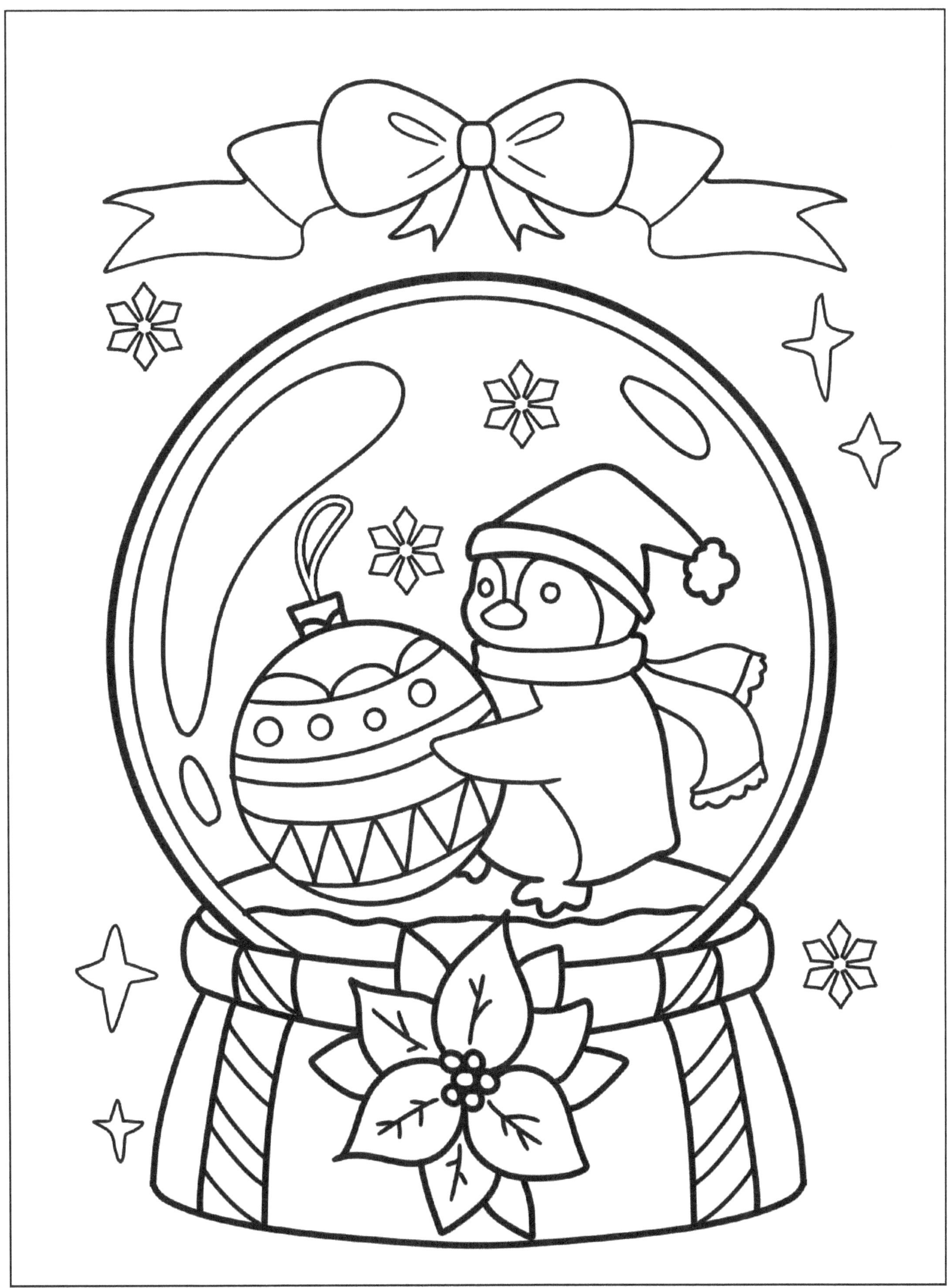

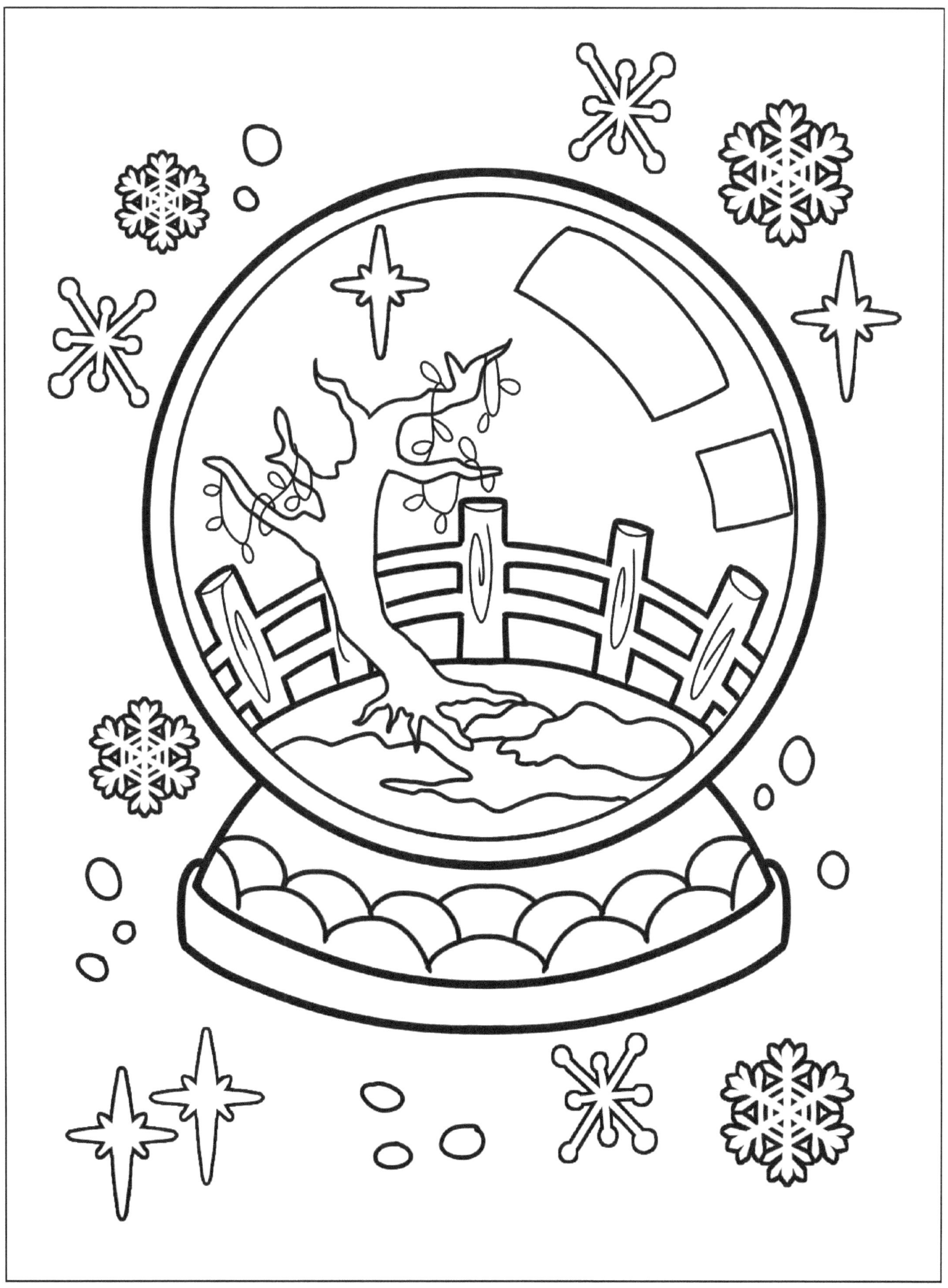

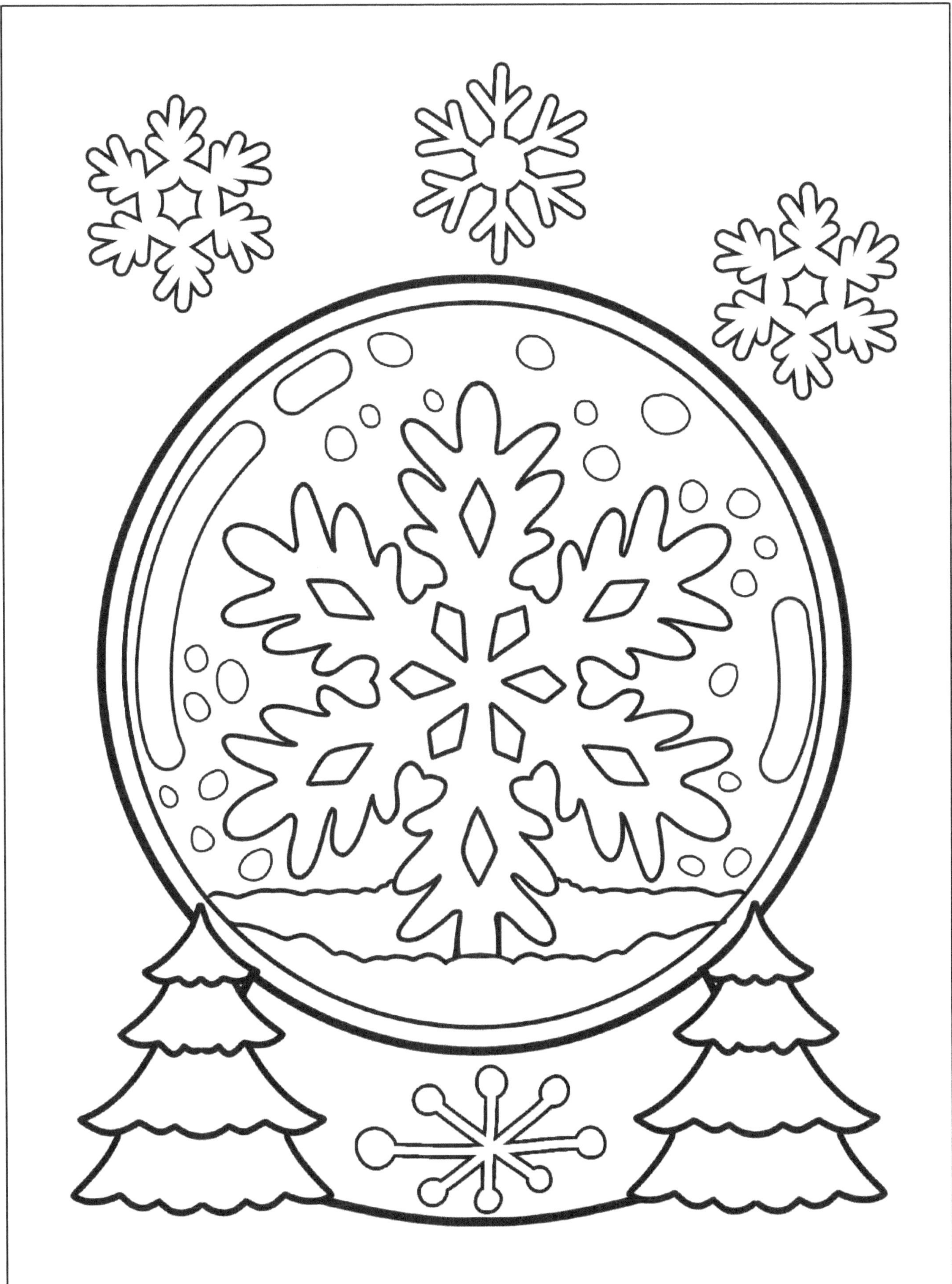

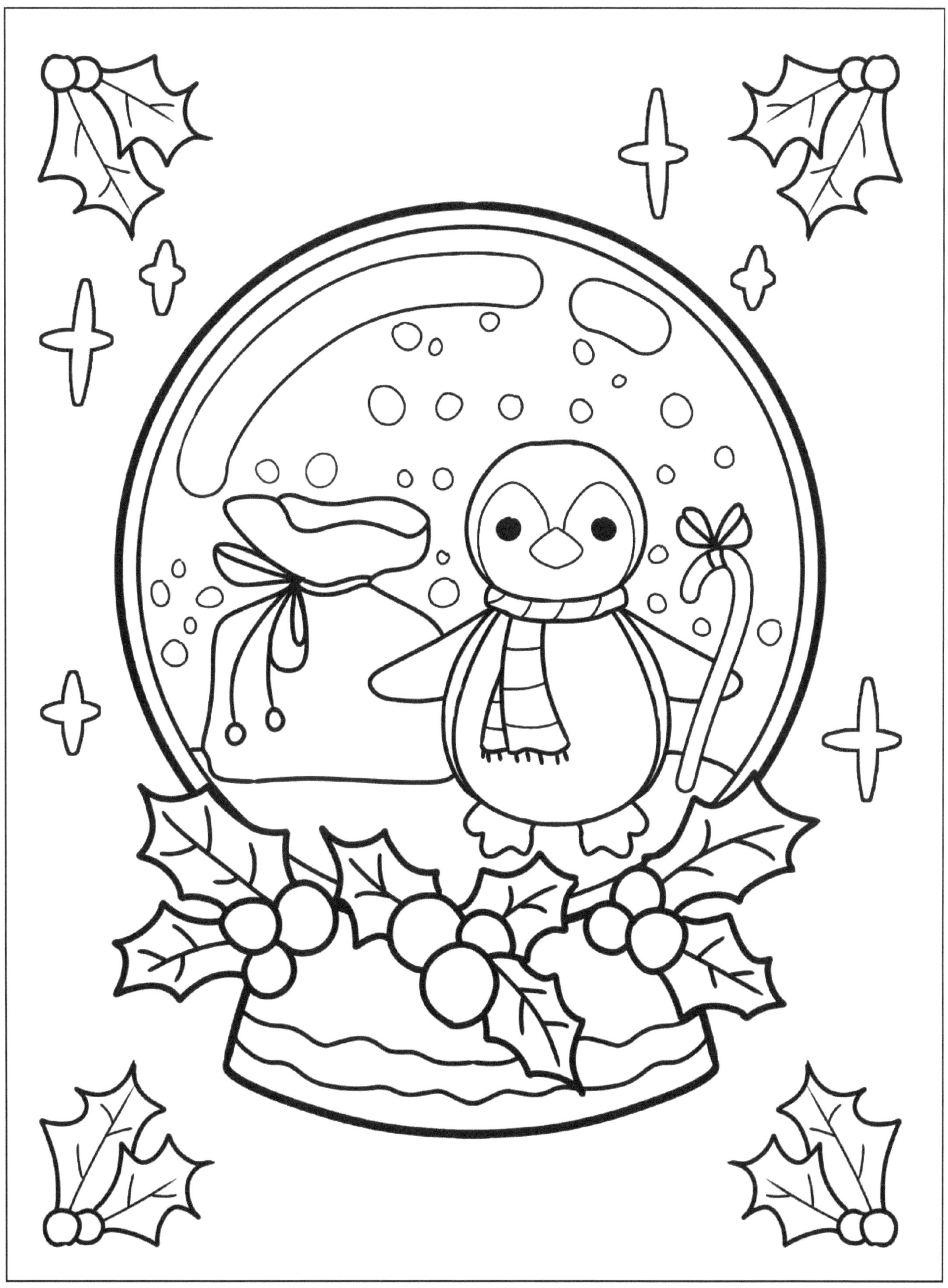

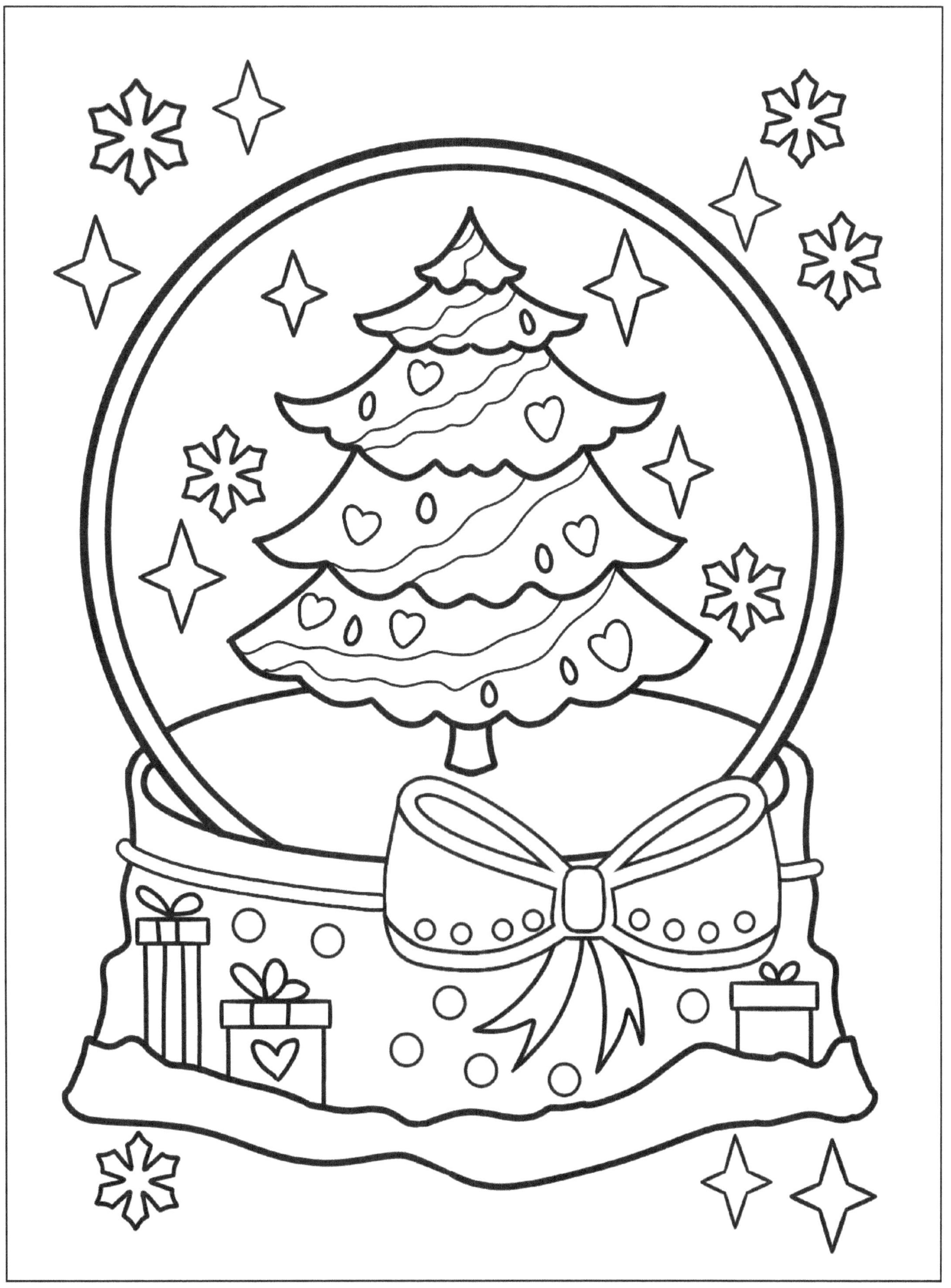

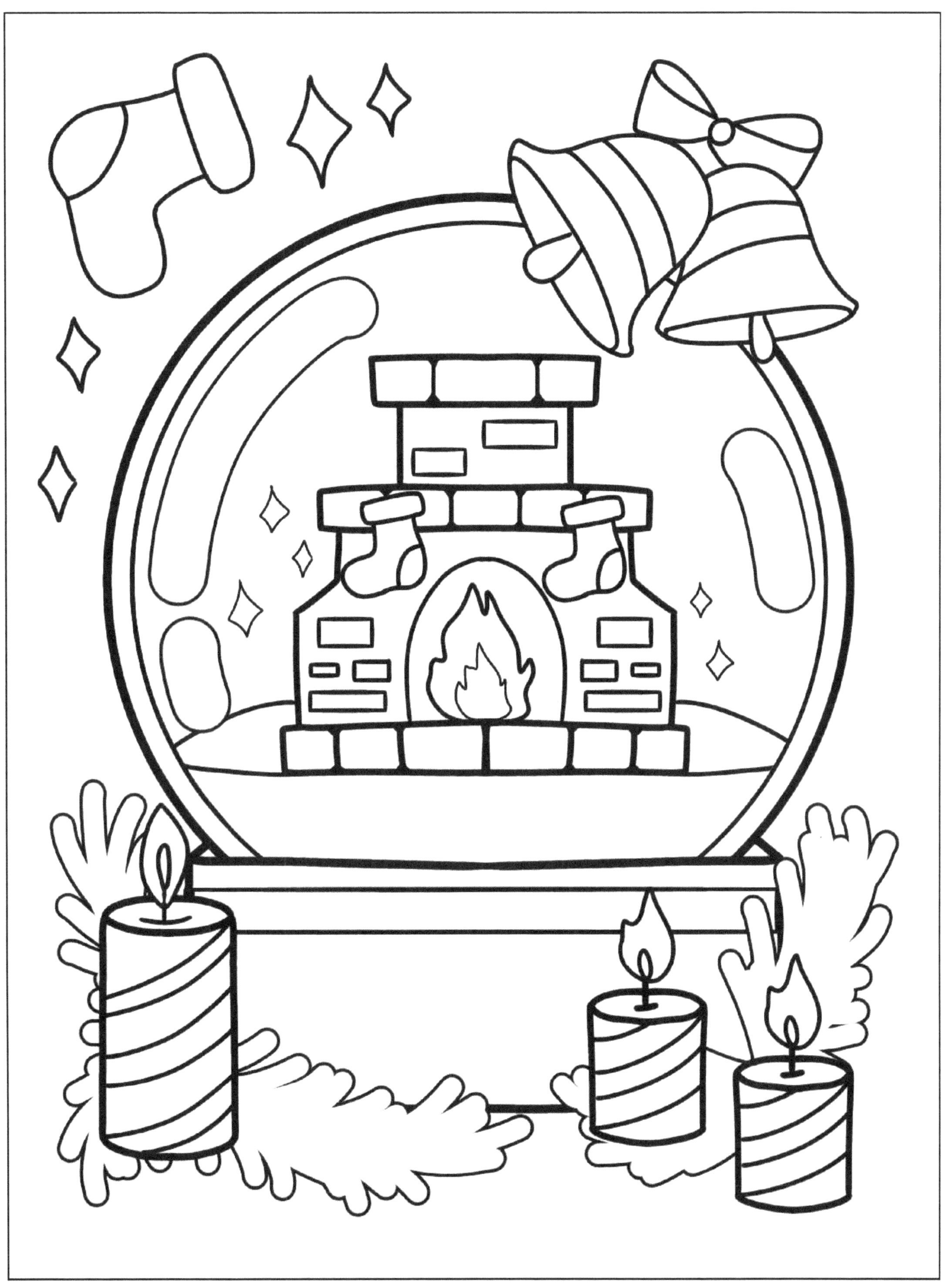

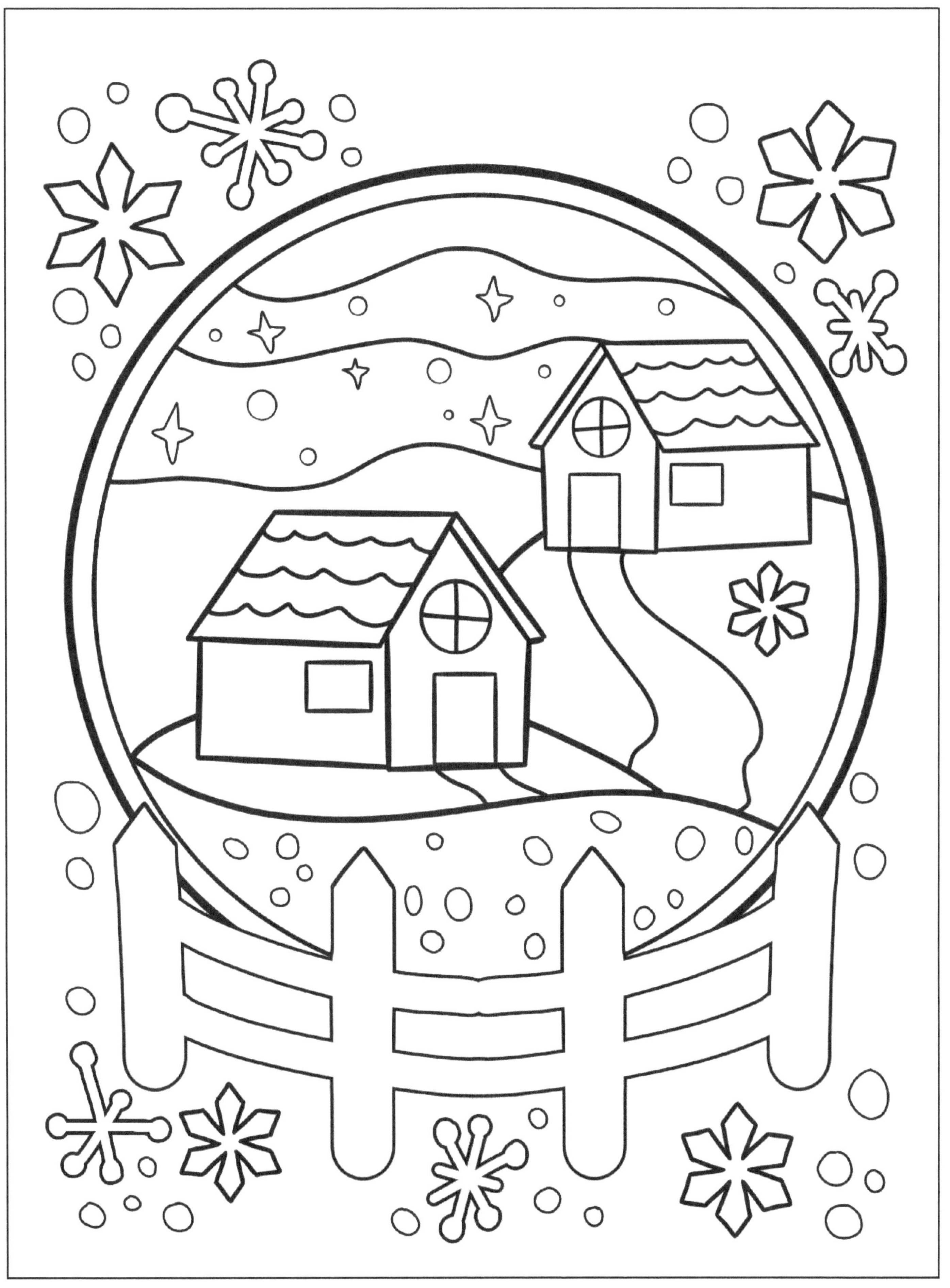

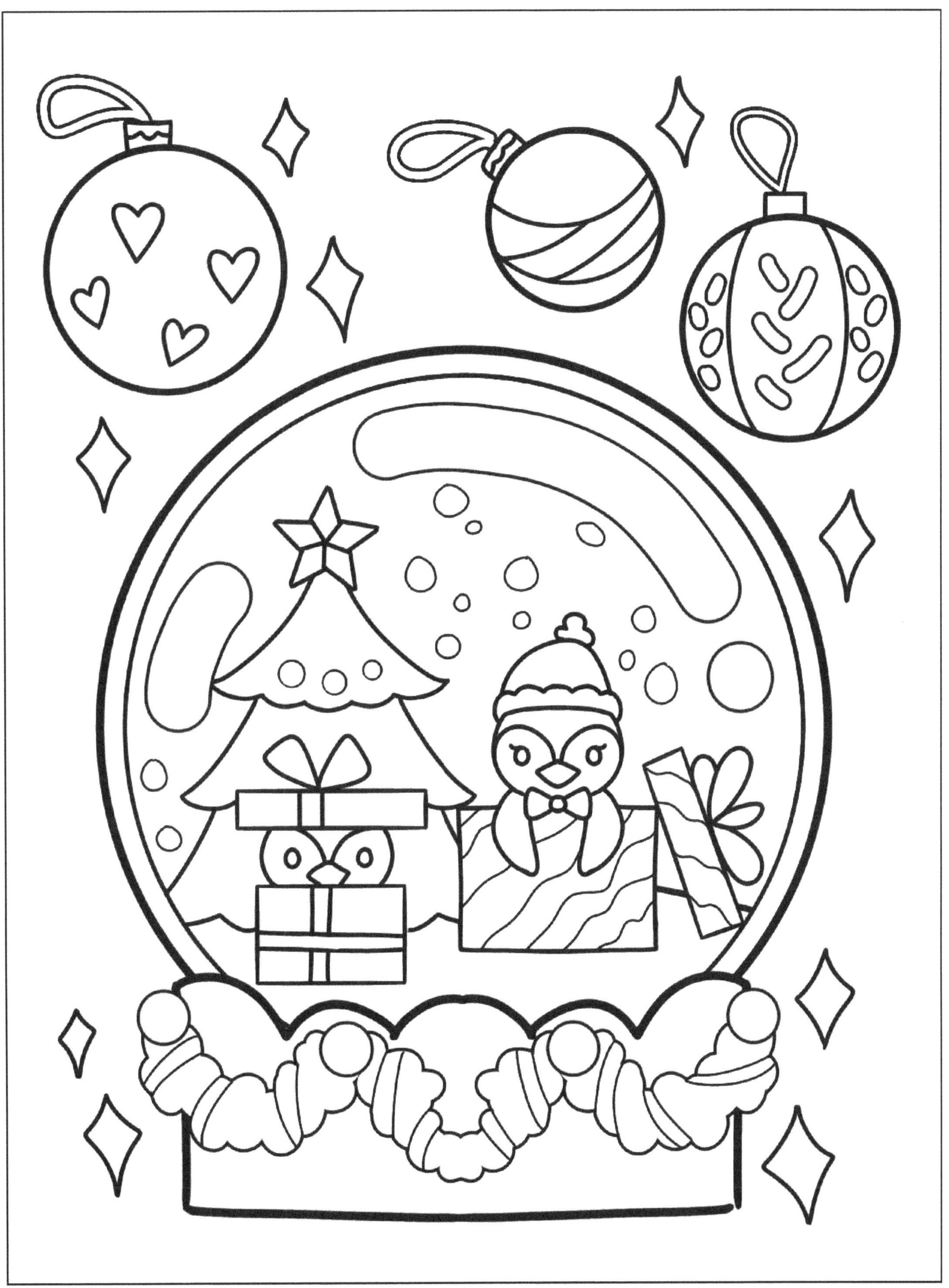

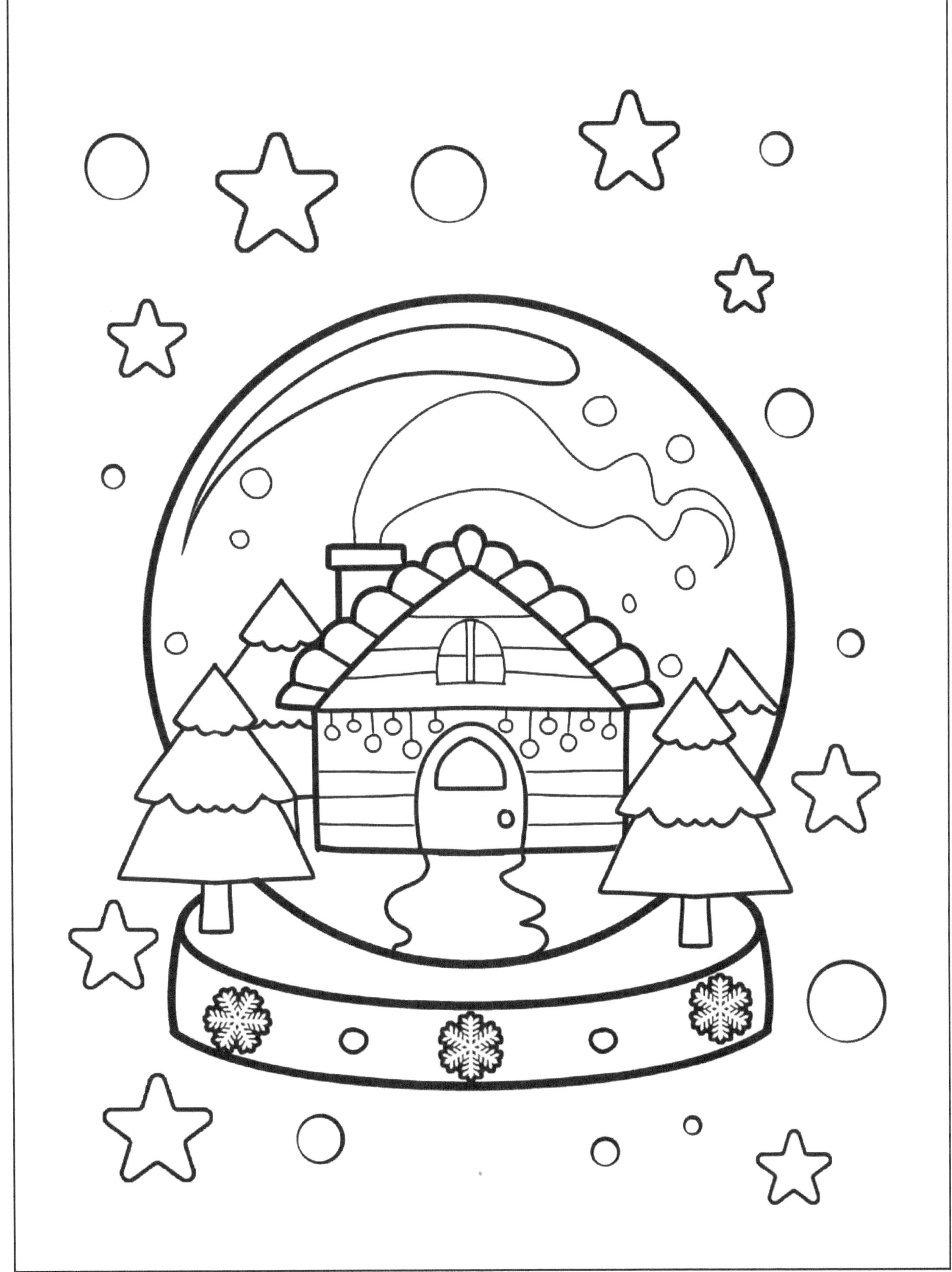

With love:

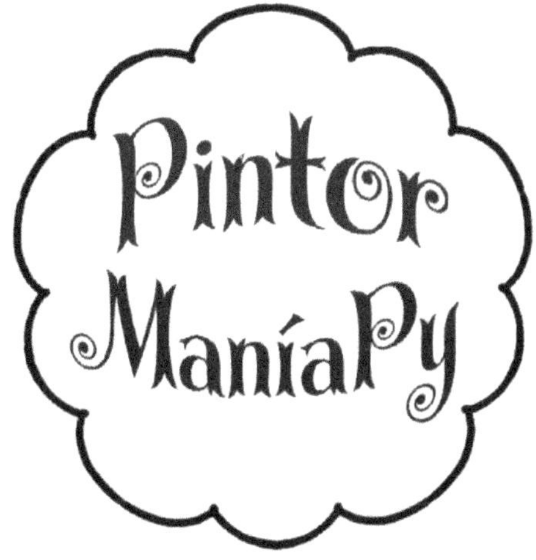